THE GREAT CHICAGO
REFUGEE RESCUE

THE GREAT CHICAGO
REFUGEE RESCUE

Picton Press

RAYMOND LOHNE

First Printing August 1997
Second Printing March 2001

This book is available from:

Picton Press
PO Box 250
Rockport, ME 04856-0250

Visa/MasterCard orders:
1-207-236-6565
FAX orders: 1-207-236-6713
e-mail: sales@pictonpress.com
Internet secure credit card orders: www.pictonpress.com

Manufactured in the United States of America
Printed on 60# acid-free paper

For Laura, my beloved wife.

The terrible thing that the Party had done was to persuade you that mere impulses, mere feelings, were of no account, while at the same time robbing you of all power over the material world. When once you were in the grip of the Party, what you felt or did not feel, what you did or refrained from doing, made literally no difference. Whatever happened you vanished, and neither you nor your actions were ever heard of again. You were lifted clean out of the stream of history. And yet to the people of only two generations ago, this would not have seemed all important, because they were not attempting to alter history. They were governed by private loyalties which they did not question. What mattered were individual relationships, and a completely helpless gesture, an embrace, a tear, a word spoken to a dying man, could have value in itself. The proles, it suddenly occurred to him, had remained in this condition. They were not loyal to a party or a country or an idea, they were loyal to one another.

Orwell
1984

AMERICAN AID SOCIETIES

- BULLETIN -

Published by the American Aid Societies

For the Needy and Displaced Persons of Central and Southeastern Europe.

| Vol. 1. No. 3 | NOVEMBER - 1948 | CHICAGO, ILLINOIS |

Courtesy American Aid Society

Cover: Original masthead drawing, artist unknown,
American Aid Societies Bulletin, November 1948.

CONTENTS

FOREWORD

Why would any American want to rescue Germans from suffering in 1944? Weren't they the enemy?

For German-Americans, such questions were no easier to answer during World War II than they had been during World War I. Back then Teddy Roosevelt, and other professional super-patriots, had told them to drop their German hyphen, and they had; loyally serving in the Armed Forces, overfulfilling bond and blood drives, while silently suffering attacks on their Americanism.

Despite the assumptions of many contemporary historians, however, German-Americans did not give up their language and other aspects of their ethnic culture. Pearl Harbor, and Hitler's declaration of war on the United States, once again brought heartaches, but little equivocation on the part of the vast majority of the 20-25% of Americans whose patriotic loyalties were to America, but whose mother tongue and childhood habits sprang from German-speaking Europe. How, indeed, does one imagine the American war effort between 1941 and 1945 as possible without the full and hearty participation of one quarter or so of its population of German heritage? Without mentioning the well known higher commanders and staff officers like Eisenhower, Nimitz, Wedemeyer, and Eichelberger, one can demonstrate this common-sense observation at the troop level in Trevor N. Dupuy's recent study of the Battle of the Bulge, where numerous German names [Lauer, Koch, Sibert, Huebner, Hirschfelder, Truppner] pop out of his narrative as key officers and enlisted men on the American side.

All of the above was obvious to the men and women who put together the remarkable effort described by Raymond Lohne in *The Great Chicago Refugee Rescue 1944-1952*. This revealing volume, using the records of the American Aid Societies, documents the existence of a viable German-American political constituency in Illinois that local historians in particular and American historians in general still seem loathe to acknowledge. Most research and writing dealing with German-

American themes in the post World War II era has concentrated on events unfolding in Germany [the Nuremberg Trials, the Morganthau Plan, the Berlin Airlift, for example] and their impact on Americans as a whole, without any particular concern for a German-American constituency. Such an approach leaves little room for the idea that German-Americans might have been as interested, vocal, and influential concerning events in Europe as, say, Polish-Americans, Greek-Americans, or Jewish-Americans.

Unlike academics, and a few national politicians, Chicago Mayors from William Dever in the 1920s to Richard M. Daley in 1997 have always paid their respects to "the German vote." Also, it is a rare German-American occasion in the Chicago area that does not see a representative from Illinois Governor Jim Edgar. And in his post election analysis of Harry Truman's upset victory over Thomas Dewey in 1948, Sam Lubbell concluded that it was the shift in German-American voting patterns that had decided the election:

> In view of the closeness of the 1948 election, the German-American swing can definitely be credited with giving Truman his margin of victory... German-Americans all over the country shifted together, as if in response to some subconscious instinct...[it]...was largely a revolt of German-American farmers against involvement in war with Germany. With the war's end and Roosevelt's passing, many of these same farmers returned to the Democratic fold.
>
> Nor was this...swing merely an agricultural one...surveys [for] 1940 and 1948 showed the same pattern for German-American precincts in the cities.
>
> ...Disloyalty is not involved. That should be stressed. Isolationist voters sent their sons to war and those sons served as patriotically and heroically as any Americans.[1]

The Danube Swabian-Americans in Chicago certainly did not possess any inside knowledge of a "German-American swing vote," but in their courting of politicians like Senator Everett Dirksen, and their skillful alliance with major Catholic Church lobbies in Washington, they demonstrated a sophistication that would do any contemporary advance-man proud. Although the vicissitudes of national and international politics profoundly affected their success, they left nothing to chance, and they never, ever stopped the struggle until their political goal was reached.

---

[1] Sam Lubell, *The Future of American Politics*, Garden City, N.Y.: Doubleday Anchor, 1951, 142-3.

Towards the end of his book, Mr. Lohne quotes the Schwob refugees brought over by the efforts of the American Aid Societies as somewhat disappointed that its leaders, Messrs. Pesch and Meiszner, were not from loftier positions in society than those of tailor and undertaker. How could such humble people have moved the higherups to their will? It was simply unimaginable, and, apparently, a trifle degrading for these *Volksdeutsche*. They were accustomed to an oligarchic society which would not permit such egalitarianism to prevail. Only Dukes or other "big shots" could produce such results in Europe. To be delivered by individuals of such common stock, however salutary, was like some kind of huge practical joke.

Precisely. A huge joke, but no laughing matter. In a land where Democratic Governor Huey Long of Louisiana had proclaimed "every man a King" and Republican Governor William Langer of North Dakota had declared "people are more important than profits," Danube Swabian-Americans were unafraid to pursue a promise of democratic power in the United States which was a rebuke to other hierarchical societies around the world, and quite literally unthinkable to their *Landsleute* from the Banat and the Batschka. The American-Schwobs were treading a path formerly trod by English, Irish, and Italian-Americans before them.

Simultaneously with the struggles of Nick Pesch and John Meiszner to push the buttons of American power on behalf of their Hungarian-German kinsmen, American Jews were finally flexing their political muscle on behalf of Israel abroad and an end to the anti-semitism that still resonated throughout American society. Among its other virtues, a unique contribution of this book is to show that American political and bureaucratic obstacles to the immigration of Danube Swabian survivors of the *Vertreibung* [Expulsion] were often identical to those faced by Jewish survivors of the Holocaust.

In his brilliant essay "The Great Cat Massacre," Robert Darnton teaches us that when we can't quite get the joke of a certain period, we are actually getting close to the mindset of the people who were living in that time and place. In his example the time was the 1740s and the joke was on Guild Masters in a French provincial city. In Mr. Lohne's example the time is the recent past, and the joke is on all who have underestimated the efficacy of American democracy in the hearts and minds of average German-Americans. The list, I am sad to say, is a long one. A careful reading of Raymond Lohne's *The Great Chicago Refugee Rescue 1944-1952* should go a long way to reducing the numbers on that list.

                                        CHARLES M. BARBER
                  Professor of History, Northeastern Illinois University

PREFACE

This study is about a group of Hungarian-German emigrés called the Danube-Swabians who were living in Chicago at the end of the Second World War. It is an attempt to document the way they responded to the catastrophe that was engulfing their kinsmen in Hungary, Romania and Yugoslavia with the entrance of Soviet forces into these countries. That response was essentially a rescue operation which helped save thousands of *Schwobs* by first feeding and clothing them, and then by actually bringing them to America in two great waves. It is that first wave, which began in 1944 and crested in 1952, which forms the basis of this work.

To understand this remarkable feat it will be necessary to summarize the history of these *Donauschwaben*, a history both magnificent and tragic, the saga of a people struggling to live in what was for them an empty land, fertile and rich with possibilities. It is the story of a people who came to the middle basin of the Danube in the 17th century and who fled it, after two and a half centuries of back-breaking labor, as desperate refugees. It was these forlorn masses that the *American Aid Societies for the Needy and Displaced Persons of Central and Southeastern Europe* sought to save.

Rescues are revealed in myriad forms, as varied as human need and as ordinary as human circumstance can become, and most do not take on the proportions of paramount catastrophe, rather, they are acted out in that almost hidden realm of unexceptional, everyday life. This effort was born out of the shattering maelstrom of the Second World War in Europe and yet unfolded within the confines of the American existence, working itself out in a practical, characteristically American way.

The event I have chosen to call the Great Chicago Refugee Rescue was both the work of the collective body of *Ungarndeutsche* in Chicago and other cities, and the efforts of certain exceptional, impassioned individuals. It amounted to Germans rescuing Germans from within an anti-German environment. The Hungarian-Germans of Chicago, in order to rescue their people in Eastern Europe, may be said to have become 'more American' to accomplish it. This event cannot claim completely unique status, for there was another German-for-German rescue effort in Chicago that followed a great upheaval and ended up working out in an interestingly American manner.

This precedent can be related by the story of Dr. Stromberg's horse, found in boxes of crumbling and yellowed documents which are all that remain of what was one of the oldest organized charities in Chicago. It is glued into a scrapbook of newspaper clippings, compiled by some diligent secretary, which are so fragile that simply turning the pages results in some disintegration. Unveiling the cheap, brittle cardboard and Gothic newsprint reveals fragmentary snapshots in the life of the German Aid Society of Chicago, although each page pried open makes the archivists at the Special Collections Department of the Library of the University of Illinois at Chicago wince a little bit.

This grimacing is bittersweet though, because reading through this scrapbook means that the destructive and constructive acts combine. To examine these documents there is no alternative to opening them and in that process some portion crumbles into powder. Fortunately, in this case, the greater part remains. From the dust to the disc the story of Dr. Stromberg's horse passes on.

In the winter of 1873 it appears that the 'collection committees' of the Society were having trouble soliciting donations. It was a typical winter in Chicago, the only difference being that the city had been ravaged by the Great Fire two years before. The world-wide outpouring of aid to the stricken city had apparently come to an end and this was making it especially hard on the 'inmates' of the German Home For The Shelterless at 140 North Union Street, which the German Aid Society owned. In fact, it was a terrible time to be at the North Union house. Food and clothing donations had nearly ceased. According to the anonymous writer of the clipping, the men were wearing 'rags infested with vermin', the only clothing donation they had received being two suits which belonged to a man who had hanged himself a few weeks before.

It was in this context of deprivation that a certain Dr. Stromberg benevolently donated a horse to the lodging house, or at any rate an animal that resembled a horse. To begin with, it appears the beast was definitely lame in all four legs. It had suffered the indignity of having its tail cropped. There wasn't a tooth in the poor creature's head, which necessitated a diet of 'soft feed', and finally, there was scarcely a patch of hair anywhere to be found on it's bony body. The unknown writer tells us:

> It is useless to say that as a draft-horse he is not a success, and as an ornament is not needed. But the Society, however, has hit upon a method of using the horse to great advantage. It is employed as a solicitor for aid for the lodging house. The horse is put in a light wagon every morning, and a Professor's son, who is at present unemployed, drags it around to the various German butcher-shops and bakeries. The Professor's son enters the place and asks for a donation, but is not only refused, but also insulted. He then tells them to look at his horse, which request they usually comply with. What the emaciated and hungry Professor's son could not accomplish, the poor, shivering half-dead animal does at once. 'For God's sake', they say, 'take away this horse from the front of our shop before it dies; we will give you anything you ask, but drive it away and do not ruin our business by such a sight.' Yesterday, one butcher was so overcome with emotion by looking at the animal that he donated an entire hog to the Society, and, for this feat, the horse was munificently rewarded with a new pair of irons worth $4. Mr. Emil Dietsch, the Superintendent of the dispensary, thinks a great deal of this horse, and if it should die would be inconsolable for the loss.[2]

There is an aspect of humor in this, even though men were starving, freezing, subject to disease and even death. We may chuckle because we know that this is begging of the most calculated kind, pitiful and thereby practically perfect. This street-wise, hard-boiled strategy of rescue is a poignant example of the Chicago-colored style these German-American rescuers adopted. It almost seems as if the tactics 'fit' in this rough and tumble American city. Seventy-one years later the *Ungarndeutsche* of Chicago would also use a calculated, practically perfect form of begging to help their countrymen. They would use American politics.

---

[2] Scrapbook, 1873-1896. Folder 156, *German Aid Society Records*, Department of Special Collections, Library of the University of Illinois at Chicago.

ACKNOWLEDGEMENTS

This study originated in the disheveled Memory-Hole office of a pugnacious, politically active Princetonian who teaches history at Northeastern Illinois University, named Charles M. Barber. Like most such intimate collaborative processes between a graduate student and his thesis advisor, the focus of this study is the result of his teaching about the *kleine Leute* and their relationship to the elites of the world. It was his work and his fascination with the 'Orwellian overtones' of these 'proles' who always seemed to be squeezed between Big Brothers such as the Austrian and Ottoman Empires; or the Magyar and the German ruling classes; or Hitler and Stalin that directly led me to this small and relatively unknown group of people.

In the process of documenting their story, Charlie Barber was wise enough to send me to see Professor Leo Schelbert of the University of Illinois at Chicago, a methodical Swiss scholar whose love for immigrants is matched only by his gentle and Socratic style. His careful, guiding hand must also be acknowledged in this work. For everything they have taught me, I claim them both as my mentors.

Many other people took the time to share their experiences with me, either under the probing duress of the audio-taped interview or the glaring lights of video camera equipment, and their efforts are hereby gratefully acknowledged. These interviews are the seeds of a future archive of survivor's stories which will be housed at the University of Illinois at Chicago.

In particular I would like to thank Eve Koehler for the time and materials she graciously gave me. I must also thank Richard Gunther and Helen Meiszner for their extensive work in behalf of this study. Their recollections were pivotal in the reconstruction of this story. Helen Meiszner's personal collection of documents and photographs were absolutely critical and I humbly thank both her and her daughter Joyce for their help.

I want to thank the American Aid Society for granting me use of their documents, especially Joe Stein, the current Secretary of the A.A.S. It was Stein, himself a survivor of the Yugoslavian death-camps, who first collected and then catalogued the incredible cache of documents that form the foundation of this work. The following people also contributed to making this book possible. Hans and Betty Gebavi, Walter Scheffran, Otmar Kapfhammer, Angela Stumpfoll, Helen and Nick Fritz, Leni and Nick Ippach, Jacob Horvath, Emmi Koch, Adam Beckloff, Katherine Glasenhardt, Martin Istl, Rolf Albrecht, Peter Krebs, Bruno Reichert and Stefan Hehn. I must also acknowledge Dr. Joseph Morton, as well as Dr. Craig Smith, Dr. Fred MacDonald and Dr. Greg Singleton.

I have to acknowledge my loving friends and family, especially Michael Steinberg, the literary agent who forced me to give up my romantic old typewriter for a computer, John and Gwen Miller, who bought me my first computer, my father, Ortwin Lohne, who immediately took it apart, and Patricia Helga Lohne, who showed me some of its secrets. I deeply thank Laura Miller Lohne for typing this entire manuscript at least ten times and hearing it read to her innumerable times. I must thank Lewis Bunker Rohrbach for his extensive efforts on this manuscript. I want to thank my supporters, especially my mother Marianne, and her husband Ted Moreland, my baby sister Monica and her gentle giant Rodney Floyd, Franceso and Amy Arena, Kenny and Cassie Miller, George and Carol Gill, Jutta Lohne, Ed and Tracey Sands, Jimmy and Nancy Sands, Tyrone, Sherry and Tommy Anderson, and my best man, Al Newton. I must acknowledge the host of nieces and nephews whose presence brightens my life, especially Sarah Arena, my *bella bambina*, my beloved Jason, and my cherished stepson, Welton, who never read a word of any of this.

Lastly, I want to thank the Gateway Foundation, without which none of this would have been possible.

Raymond Arthur Lohne
Chicago, Illinois
June 1997

PROLOGUE

UBI POPULUS, IBI OBULUS[3]

1686-1829: The Migrations

The people who eventually came to be called the Danube-Swabians generally begin their history in 1683 with the final Turkish siege of Vienna, which ended with an irreversible Ottoman defeat. For the next three decades the Muslims would be driven southeast, out of Hungary, down into the Balkans, leaving behind a land fertile but neglected. For 150 years it had been little more than a foraging ground, battlefield and staging area for attacks into the heart of Christian Europe. The Ottomans extracted all that they could during their occupation and this left the victorious Hapsburg Monarchy with a barren territory. This is land the Hungarians and the Austrians were naturally eager to repopulate.

To the Danube-Swabians it is important that historians recognize their claim that the Hungarians wanted them in Hungary first. In a small collaborative and self-published pamphlet, three Swabian writers, Anton Tafferner, Josef Volkmar Senz, and Josef Schmidt argue that it was the Magyar landed gentry who immediately and privately sought colonists to work their recovered estates. Significant to them is the fact that

> ...it is not Austria, but rather the Hungarian nobility -clerical and temporal-who first encouraged colonization. The Hapsburgs were busy with the Turkish and French wars until 1718... After the Peace of Passarowitz (1718) the Imperial (Austrian) court and defense council (military border) joined this private colonization with a more benevolent and modern means of settling.[4]

For a people who were expelled *en masse* it is apparently critical to establish that they were wanted in the beginning. Although the *Donau-*

---

[3] Where there are people, there is wealth.

[4] Anton Tafferner, Josef Schmidt, Josef Senz, *The Danube-Swabians in the Pannonian Basin: A New German Ethnic Group*. (Danube-Swabian Association, USA, Inc., 1982), 8.

schwaben, as a distinct ethnic group, begin their story here, historical scholarship recognizes the much earlier presence of Germans in Hungary. Geza Paikert noted that as early as the eleventh century

> ...we see in Hungary the familiar pattern so characteristic of the whole of east-central and a great part of eastern Europe: the industrious, frugal and capable Germans come to constitute the core of burgherdom in the emerging cities. The city-building excellence of the Germans, who for centuries virtually monopolized that trade in Hungary, was eloquently given credit by the noted eighteenth century historian Bel Matyas (Mathias Belius). Paul Hunfalvy, a later Hungarian historian of the nineteenth century, noted fittingly that 'the Magyars established in Hungary the state, the Germans built the cities'.[5]

The history of the re-colonization of Hungary cannot simply be seen through Swabian eyes. In his analysis of a similar migratory situation, that of the founding of winegrowing settlements in Vevay, Indiana and Chabag, Russia at the turn of the 19th century, Leo Schelbert wrote:

> In sum, the making of Vevay in America and Chabag in Russia shows that human migration is shaped by a complex interplay of personal concerns and the aims of statecraft. Most often individual goals did not include escape from bad conditions, but the search for leadership as for Tardent, the hope for a place in history as for John James Dufour, or the winegrowers' quest for elemental satisfaction that derived from the transference of a familiar pursuit like viticulture into new domains. As long as immigrants felt assured, furthermore, that they could pursue their personal goals unimpeded on the familial, village and district level, they readily gave allegiance to a republican as well as an autocratic polity. They embraced, finally, reasons of state such as the dislocation or encirclement of indigenous peoples unhesitatingly as their own as their communities seemed threatened by indigenous strategies of resistance. This made the newcomers not only architects of their own personal, familial, and communal destinies, but also partners in the pursuit of national goals as defined by governmental elites. The private and the public, the personal and the collective quests thus were inseparably to merge.[6]

1723-1726: The Karolinian Migration

For the Swabians this confluence of personal desires and the Empire's aims began when Austria started a systematic effort, at the

---

[5] Geza Paikert, *The Danube-Swabians: German Populations in Hungary, Rumania and Yugoslavia and Hitler's Impact on their Patterns.* (The Hague: Martinus Nijhoff, 1967), 20.

[6] Leo Schelbert, "Vevay, Indiana, and Chabag, Bessarabia: The Making of Two Winegrowers Settlements". *Yearbook of German-American Studies*, Vol. 25, (1990), 109.

request of the Hungarian Parliament of 1723, to lure as many young Catholic couples as possible for the reimpopulation effort. The first mass migration occurred during the reign of Charles VI. In a short monograph on this topic Michael Bresser wrote:

> Included in this first colonization were approximately 15,000 German speaking farmers who came from the area of the Rhine river and its tributaries. They were assigned to the south-east area next to the Danube river along the Turkish border. Living in huts, toiling ceaselessly, sustained by their Catholic faith (a prerequisite to immigration), they succeeded in making the rich soil nourish their crops and with one tenth of the harvest pay the government taxes. They were the forefathers of the Danube-Swabians.[7]

Although some went by land, the majority of the colonists traveled down the Danube in large box-like boats, going through Imperial processing in Vienna before continuing. Downriver their boats squeezed out between the Alps and the edge of the Carpathian Mountains before entering the Little Hungarian Plain. For about 100 miles they headed east, escaping through the Carpathians again at Esztergom. At Vac, Hungary, where the river heads south and begins its slow meandering through 230 miles of the Great Hungarian Plain they found themselves entering an immense alluvial valley, constantly subject to the violent flooding of the mighty river.

DEUTSCHE ANSIEDLER IM UNTEREN DONAURAUM

Der große Schwabenzug
XVIII. JAHRHUNDERT

NACH EINEM ÖLBILD VON STEFAN JÄGER

Der Große Schwabenzug

---

[7] Michael Bresser, *The Danube-Swabians: Biography of a People from Inception to Dispersal.* (Philadelphia, Pa.: Danube-Swabian Association, no date), 3.

Art as historical narrative. On the prior page is *Der Grosse Schwabenzug*, a painting by Stefan Jager depicting the apportioning of homesites. Source: Swabian pamphlet. Below is *Ulmer Schachtel*, a painting by Sebastion Leicht depicting the barge-like boats used by people to migrate down the river. Source: Sebastion Leicht, *Weg der Donauschwaben: Dreihundert Jahre Kolonistenschicksal, Graphischer Zyklus*. (Passau: Verlag Passavia, 1983), 53.

Ulmer Schachtel

This was also the region of the rebuilt *Österreichische Militärgrenze*, now called the *Gränitz*, which served as a protective buffer zone of defensive farm settlements. This was essentially a no-man's land, where generations of:

> ...strong and brave but rather primitive and unruly peoples had spent their entire lives in a never-ending, gruesome guerilla warfare against their Moslem tormentors.[8]

---

[8] Geza Paikert, *The Danube-Swabians*, 20.

It is fair to say that these people had been imported into a combat zone. Paikert goes a step further.

> The colonists, notwithstanding the immeasurable help they received...had not come to Hungary with the reassuring expectation of living in a placid Canaan, abundant with milk and honey. It is to their credit that they were fully aware of the extremely harsh conditions which were to face them in their new home land, at that time much more desolate and beset with lurking danger than the North American West ever was for the immigrant pioneers of the late nineteenth century.[9]

In his pictorial history entitled *The Banat Germans*, Nikolaus Engelmann provides a raw, nakedly vivid description of the land as he viewed it in 1961. We can imagine what these early pioneers saw when they climbed out of their huge, flat-bottomed rafts 238 years earlier, in 1723.

> As one approaches the Banat heartland, whether through the heath or across the sand of the south, the appearance is one of monotonous desolation. The roads and highways stretch far into the distance, unadorned by trees or bushes. In the summertime a glimmering heat hovers over the land. The earth has been transformed into an ankle-deep layer of fine dust that forms into huge clouds when disturbed.
>
> Along the roadsides, pitiful plants, covered over again and again with dust, thirst for rain. When the rain does come, the dust is then transformed into a dark paste into which the horses and wagons sink as the rainy season continues.[10]

Another difficult feature of the Great Hungarian Plain was the large swamps and marshlands which had to be drained, both to recover arable land, and to try checking malaria, cholera, and other diseases. Whatever the colonists' first impressions were, they went through their assigned homesites, surveying the ruins left by the retreating Turks and gauging the nature of the soil with the practiced eyes of farmers. They were of hardy peasant stock. Accepting the land with its attendant dangers, they hunkered down and survived their first winter on the wind-swept and inhospitable plain.

---

[9] Ibid., 26.
[10] Nikolaus Engelmann, *The Banat Germans*. Translated by John M. Michels. (Freilassing/Bayern: Pannonia-Verlag, 1987), 28.

The Magyar ruling classes and the Viennese Imperial Council were undoubtedly aware that they were placing these people directly astride the invasion route into Europe, and in 1738 the Turks came back through the *Gränitz*. They stormed into the Banat, enjoying easy plundering of peasant villages, having their military revenge, carrying off slaves, and putting the fresh new settlements to the torch. With this invasion the *cordon sanitaire* was ruptured, breaking Europe's only quarantine seal against the dread Bubonic plague. Many of those whom the Muslims did not massacre or enslave were wiped out by the epidemic which followed. The majority of the settlements were destroyed, and when peace was finally won in 1739, the Turkish border was so close that these settlements were not rebuilt. The first *Schwabenzug* had ended in death and disaster.

1763-73: The Theresian Migration

By 1747 the Banat of Hungary was militarily back in Austrian hands although sporadic Turkish raiding still occurred. In the German lands the word spread that "Hungary was the grave of the Germans".[11] The Empire countered this bad press with offers of light taxation, free lumber to build homes and other kinds of governmental assistance for settlers, like 'advance seed' to start a crop.[12] The campaign by Empress Maria Theresa was extensive, advertising all over the realm, and this time colonists even came from inside Austria as well as Northern and Western Hungary. They also came from Bohemia, Moravia, Silesia, Swabia, Bavaria, the Black Forest region and Westphalia. The largest group of immigrants poured out of the areas west of the Rhine, the Palatinate, the Mosel and Saar river regions and especially from Alsace and Lorraine.

This second phase of *der Grosse Schwabenzug* is said by the Swabians to have been the one which defined the character of the region for the next two hundred years. Maria Theresa's father, Charles VI had been successful in his effort to get the Hungarian nobles to accept the Pragmatic Sanction, which decreed that his daughter could inherit his dominions. When Maria Theresa did ascend to the throne she repaid the

---

[11] Bresser, p.5

[12] Josef Senz, *Bilder aus der Geschichte der Donauschwaben.* (Salzburg: Donauschwäbische-Verlaggesellschaft m.b.H., 1955), 9.

gentry in Hungary with a free hand and exemption from taxation. This period is viewed by the Danube-Swabians as a time of 'great need' because as mere peasants on lands which did not belong to them they were still vulnerable and easy to exploit. What wasn't simply taken from them by the magnates was subject to loss either from mismanagement or unfair administrative arrangements.

They claim their ancestors were victimized by the monopoly the Empire enjoyed over supplies they needed, the orders the Empire issued concerning what to grow and when, and the demands made on them to work on military fortifications, drainage canals and other projects related to the rebuilding of a viable civilization.

Furthermore, because of the debt Maria Theresa owed to the Hungarian nobles, the Danube-Swabians felt they had little hope of any redress in Vienna. As they are still proud of pointing out, the *Schwobs* worked on, surviving, even thriving in spite of the difficulties. Soon they began to create a veritable 'agricultural Eden' out of the neglected land, playing the pivotal role in transforming the region into the 'bread basket' of southeastern Europe, although it wasn't their generation that would live to eat from it.

1782-87: The Josephinian Migration

The last mass migration of German-speaking peoples occurred during the reign of Joseph II. It is thought that nearly 60,000 gathered in Ulm and Regensburg to clamber aboard massive rafts for the trip down the Danube. Government recruiters, newspaper advertising, letters from settlers and 'word of mouth' worked together to spread the story of freedom and prosperity in the southeast portion of the Empire. Jacob Steigerwald estimates that:

Approximately 150,000 German settlers took up residence in Hungary during the 143-year period from 1686 until 1829. In the Banat alone about 70,000 Germans had settled in 104 villages and towns by 1787. Approximately 1,000 German villages were established as a result of the re-impopulation efforts in Hungary.[13]

The Danube-Swabians call this last period the time of 'bread' primarily because the long peace of Maria's reign had given the farmers time to rebuild and work the fertile land. It had also given them time to fall in love with it.

38. Dorfpläne von Perjamofch und Deutfchfanttpeter a. d. Marofch.

(Ausfchnitte a. Blatt 5566 b. Karte b. Ung. Königl. Staatl. Landesaufnahme 1 : 75 000 n. b. Aufn. v. 1881 m. Rachtr. v. 1912)
Perjamofch und Deutfchfanttpeter gehören zu den älteften dt. Siedlungen des Banats. Sie entftanden im Zuge der erften großen ländl. An-
iedlung von Deutfchen zwifchen 1722 u. 1726 u. wurden beide zwifchen 1763 u. 64 bei Wiederaufnahme der ftaatl. Anfiedlungstätigleit unter
Maria Therefia erweitert (¶IV. 2 u. Karte 29 u. 30). Grundriß u. Straßennetz zeigen noch nicht die planvoll geometrifchen Formen, wie fie
päter im hügelland u. auf der heide entwidelt wurden. Perjamofch hatte 1920 5193Ew., dar. 4397 Dt.; Deutfchfanttpeter 2582 Ew., dar.1995 Dt.

Source: *Handwörterbuch des Grenz und Auslanddeutschtums*, 241

Maps showing the ordered layout of Danube-German villages

---

[13] Jacob Steigerwald, *Donauschwäbische Gedankenskizzen aus USA*. (Winona, Minn., 1983), 10-11.

Deutfche Befiedlung des Banats unter Maria Therefia.

Source: Carl Petersen, et al., *Handwörterbuch des Grenz und Auslanddeutschtums.*
(Breslau: Ferdinand Hirt, 1936), 225.

Settlement map of the Banat region

Even a cursory reading of Danube-Swabian literature confronts one
with the deep and mystical attachment these people had to *Mutterboden*
and *Landsleute*. In poetic works such as Eve Eckert Koehler's *Seven
Susannah's: Daughters of the Danube,* this sense of spiritual connected-
ness to people and homeland is poignantly expressed.[14]

---

[14] Eve Eckart Koehler, *Seven Susannahs: Daughters of the Danube.* (U.S.& Canadian
Danube Swabian Society: 1976).

The *Schwobs* seem to be great lovers of poetry, indeed one of their greatest heroes is the poet and writer Adam Müller-Guttenbrunn (1852-1923), whom Josef Senz calls the *Erzschwabe*, and it is with a poem that they teach their children, to this very day, the history of their great migrations.[15] The poem says simply:

> *Die Ersten fanden den Tod,*
> *Die Zweiten litten Not;*
> *Erst die Dritten hatten Brot!*

> The first found death,
> the second found dearth;
> only the third found bread!

Photo courtesy Helen Meiszner

Swabians enjoying folk-dancing, Chicago, ca. 1956.

---

[15] Josef Senz, *Bildcr aus der Geschichte der Donauschwaben.* (Freilassing-Bayern: Gemeinschaftsverlag Pannonia-Verlag, Donauschwäbische-Verlaggesellschaft m.b.H., Salzburg, 1955), 18.

Photo courtesy Helen Meiszner

Swabians enjoying folk-dancing, Chicago, ca. 1956.

With great love there is correspondingly great grief, and the more the *Donauschwaben* immersed themselves in their new homeland, the greater the potential for disaster. While they concerned themselves with their crops and animals, storm clouds were gathering; while they attended to each other in small, meticulously-planned villages the old world was crumbling into chaos all around them.

This is in brief outline the story of the Danube-Swabian entrance into Hungary. They did not technically even emigrate, for the land to which they went was part of the Austrian Empire. Moreover, they were enticed to come and found themselves reclaiming a wasted land in a war zone, a difference that will stamp a deep impression upon the collective psyche of these people, especially as their drama unfolds. The understructure of their subsequent tragedy is that they were simple, uncomplicated people trying to exist in a world which was to become extremely complicated. They had been asked to rebuild a land which would later become their killing field.

Photo: author

Swabian peasant scene painted by Peter Kraemer,
pictured here, himself a rescued Schwob and
survivor of the death camp at Rudolphsgnad.

CHAPTER ONE

THE TERRIBLE THING THE PARTY HAD DONE

On September 17, 1944, the *Chicago Tribune* announced in triumphant block letters

YANKS OPEN WAY TO RHINE....

This is the very day the Chicago *Schwobs* claim for the founding of the Hungarian-German Aid Society, which actually had been created in the basement of a sympathetic Croat. At this basement meeting were the leaders of the United Social Clubs of the Hungarian-Germans of Chicago, which had been formed in 1940. They were there because in the beginning of August 1944 they had come into possession of a letter written by Dr. Kasper Muth of Temesvar, Romania. Dr. Muth had been a Senator in the Rumanian Parliament and the President of the *Verband der Deutschen in Rumänien.* Josef Senz fittingly called him a *Wortführer,* a title he deserved both for his work on behalf of the Danube Swabians in Romania and the effect he had on the *Schwobs* of Chicago.[16]

Source: Josef Senz, *Bilder aus der Geschichte der Donauschwaben*

Dr. Kaspar Muth,
geb. 1876

After the capitulation of Romania, Dr. Muth had found an American soldier who was a *Schwabenkind*, and pressed into his hands a letter addressed only to the 'United Austro-Hungarian Organization of North America, Chicago, Illinois.' He had been in Chicago for a 200 year anniversary celebration for the *Schwaben* of the Banat, but

---

[16] Josef Senz, p.24

1

for some reason did not have a specific address. Incredibly, it was delivered to a local barber shop where *Donauschwaben* men were known to gather, apparently on the order of Postmaster Johann Haderlein.[17]

In this letter Dr. Muth gave a grim account of the Danube-German flight from Yugoslavia, an account which was later reflected in potent eye-witness works, such as those by Wendelin Gruber,[18] Michael Nagelbach,[19] and Traudie Müller-Wlossak.[20] Seminal work on this subject remains the encyclopedic *Documents on the Expulsion of the Germans from East Central Europe,*[21] edited by Theodor Schieder, as well as the work of Alfred Maurice de Zayas.[22] This body of literature is an echo of Dr. Muth's heart-rending letter to the *Schwobs* of Chicago in August 1944. For an analysis of the history of the *Volksdeutsche* in Hungary, Romania and Yugoslavia from World War I onwards, the reader is directed to other sources, especially Geza Paikert.[23]

What is being pursued here is the history which was significant to these men. It is fair to say that their pioneering past, not the events of Hitler's brief hegemony, were what counted most to them. Although some of the *Volksdeutsche* had undoubtedly fallen under the Nazi spell and enthusiastically supported them, the Chicago *Schwobs* were concerned with the innocent, those who were now either in a desperate headlong flight from the revengeful Soviet armies or who had been unable or unwilling to leave their homes.

[17]   Written Testimony of S.J. Baumann, American Aid Society Records, Danube-Swabian Cultural Center, Lake Villa, Illinois, 1.
[18]   Wedelin Gruber, *In The Claws of the Red Dragon: Ten Years Under Tito's Heel.* (Toronto: St. Michaelswerk Pub., 1988).
[19]   Michael Nagelbach, *Heil! And Farewell: A Life in Romania, 1913-1946.* (Chicago: Adam's Press, 1986).
[20]   Traudie Muller-Wlossak, *Die Peitsche des Tito's Kommisars.* (Passau: Passavia Druckerei GmbH, 1987).
[21]   Theodor Schieder, ed. *Das Shicksal Der Deutschen in Jugoslawien.* Vol. 1, *Das Shicksal Der Deutschen in Rumanien.* Vol. 2, *Das Schicksal Der Deutschen in Ungarn.* Vol. 3. (Augsburg: Weltbild Verlag GmbH, 1994).
[22]   Alfred Maurice de Zayas, *A Terrible Revenge: The Ethnic Cleansing of the East European Germans, 1944-1950.* (New York: St. Martin's Press, 1994).
[23]   Geza Paikert, *The Danube Swabians: German Populations in Hungary, Rumania and Yugoslavia and Hitler's Impact on their Patterns.* (The Hague: Martinus Nijhoff, 1962).

Within that vengeance the innocent and guilty alike were being punished. Women and girls were being gang-raped in the name of retribution, and then, since most of the men were dead or away, were being hauled away to Russia as slave labor. Everyone of Germanic origin was expelled from their homes, literally with mere moments of notice, their property forever confiscated in a vindictive, indiscriminate 'legal' action.

In Yugoslavia, Tito's partisans took particular pleasure in vengeance because of the atrocities committed there by the Nazis. Here again it was primarily the innocent doing all the suffering, because those *Volksdeutsche* guilty of collaborating had already fled with the retreating German armies. Confronted with masses of these people, many of whom had refused to flee because they harbored no consciousness of guilt, Tito's partisans adopted the Nazi-like expedient of herding them into selected villages, which were then cordoned off. These places became slave-labor camps for those who could work, and starvation camps for those who couldn't. In these camps the Danube Germans perished by the thousands.

Thus for the *Donauschwaben* another kind of 'terrible Turks' had flooded into their beloved homeland, and a cataclysm their ancestors had experienced in 1739 was being repeated. George Kennan's lurid description of the Red Army advance into Germany is nevertheless instructive as to the tenor of the revenge the *Schwobs* were to experience. Kennan wrote:

> The disaster that befell this area with the entry of the Soviet forces has no parallel in modern European experience. There were considerable sections of it where, to judge by all existing evidence, scarcely a man, woman, or child of the indigenous population was left alive after the initial passage of Soviet forces...
> ...they had swept the native population clean in a manner that had no parallel since the days of the Asiatic hordes.[24]

These men saw this tragedy through the corrective lenses of their past, with vision focused admittedly on the simplicity and goodness of their people. Hugh Seton-Watson once said, in a lecture delivered at the University of Washington in 1973:

---

[24] George F. Kennan, *Memoirs 1925-1950*, (Boston, Little, Brown and Co., 1967), 265.

> In the 1930s in most of these countries there were two nations: a Europeanized upper stratum of perhaps 10 to 30 percent of the population, who lived and thought more or less the same way as their social counterparts in Germany or France, and the rest, who lived in an almost medieval world, ranging if you like from the eighteenth century French peasant to the nineteenth century Russian *muzhik*.[25]

These men were convinced that their *Landsleute* fell into the category of those who existed in the 'medieval world', an uncomplicated, politically unsophisticated folk who had been easily seduced by propaganda and manipulated by Nazi officials. In a recent study by Valdis O. Lumans, this aspect of the *Volksdeutsche* experience is clearly shown. Lumans even asserts that a primary motivation of the Nazis with regard to the *Volksdeutsche* must be seen within

> ...the Reich's interest in tapping this reservoir of German manpower for the Waffen SS. This enterprise, no less than that of securing Hungarian military participation in the war against the Soviet Union, depended on the good graces of Budapest. Before the Vienna Award, very few Hungarian *Volksdeutsche* enlisted in the *Waffen SS*. But as of August 1940, the *SS* exploited the officially recognized relationship between the minority and the Reich to escalate its efforts. *SS* recruiters lured young *Volksdeutsche* to the Reich on the pretext of participating in work or play. Once there, they were subjected to propaganda and military training, with an option to join the *Waffen SS*.[26]

The *Schwobs* Catch-22 position is perhaps best illustrated by the observation of Jacob Steigerwald. He explained that the *Donauschwaben*

> ...found themselves in positions of double jeopardy and no-win situations in WW II. The leaders of Hungary and Romania, for example, thought they opted for the lesser of two evils when they initially sided with Hitler, rather than with Stalin...The German minorities within these countries experienced a worse fate yet, since they were first used by the National Socialists, with the apparent consent of the host countries, and later had to endure abuses on the basis of their national origin. Being ethnic German, they had to suffer for Hitler's

---

[25] Hugh Seton-Watson, *The Sick Heart of Modern Europe: The Problem of the Danubian Lands*, (Seattle, University of Washington Press, 1975), 60.

[26] Valdis O. Lumans, *Himmler's Auxiliaries: The Volksdeutsche Mittelstelle and the German National Minorities of Europe, 1933-1945*, (Chapel Hill, Univ. of North Carolina Press, 1993), 224.

atrocities even though, as citizens of non-German states, they had neither voted him into office nor were they ever in a position to control his actions.[27]

The Chicago *Schwobs* were fully aware that this was a land and a people few Americans understood, and if America didn't know who the *Donauschwaben* were, or what their history was, they certainly wouldn't be able to generate much sympathy for them in this situation. In fact, that was already the case militarily, as Stephen D. Kertesz pointed out when he commented

> ...by this time Danubian Europe had become the dark side of the moon for the Western allies. The Joint Chiefs of Staff had decided in the autumn of 1943 that the United States should take no responsibilities 'in the area of the Balkans, including Austria'.[28]

These were the realities as the Chicago Swabian leaders saw them. The remarkable fact is that they were even meeting at all. These were overwhelming world events which they were powerless to prevent. What 'helpless gestures', to use Orwell's phrase, could they offer in the face of such catastrophe? If, as Hugh Seton-Watson taught, the job of the historian "is to understand and record moods as well as events, states of mind as well as statistics", then we should remember the mood that permeated America with regard to things German in 1944.[29] With that in view, the reason these men were meeting in a basement becomes a little clearer.

Sam Baumann was the organizer of the Charity Committee of the United Social Clubs, and the man charged with the task of getting a hall for this meeting. Everyone he approached within the Hungarian-German community bluntly refused. "Baumann..." they told him. "You'll get jailed for this." Even the Croat had a proviso to issue before letting them use his basement.

> "If the FBI wiretaps you..." he said plainly. "I'll swear I didn't know you were here."[30]

---

[27] Jacob Steigerwald, *Tracing Romania's Heterogeneous German Minority from its Origins to the Diaspora*, (Winona, Minn., Winona State University Press, 1985), v.

[28] Stephen D. Kertesz, *Between Russia and the West: Hungary and the Illusions of Peacemaking 1945-1947*, (Notre Dame, Univ. of Notre Dame Press, 1984), xii.

[29] Hugh Seton-Watson, *The Sick Heart of Modern Europe*, 27.

[30] Written testimony of Sam Baumann, American Aid Society Records.

War hysteria is a potent force, as is attested to by the treatment of Japanese-Americans after Pearl Harbor. In this conflict-poisoned mental landscape the *Schwobs* were wise to hold their meeting 'underground'. Rudolph Hofmeister observed that by 1935 the Abendpost published a roster of "at least 452 active German clubs in the Chicago area."[31] Eleven short years later these Hungarian-Germans had to meet in a Croat's basement.

The responses of those people Baumann approached shouldn't be too surprising if we remember that many of them probably still had frightening memories of anti-Germanism during World War I. A select group of scholars have done work on this facet of American history, notably Frederick C. Luebke, who documented this experience in his book *Bonds of Loyalty: German-Americans and World War I*. His work is especially riveting when he describes April 5, 1918 in Collinsville, Illinois. That was the day a German-American worker named Robert Paul Prager was lynched on suspicion of being a spy by a crowd of 'patriots' after being bizarrely paraded through town draped only with the American flag. This was the worst case, and the only authenticated example of a German being lynched, but Luebke points out that

> The Prager murder was by no means an isolated example of the hysteria that was sweeping across the nation in the spring of 1918.
> The number of German-Americans abused by superpatriots increased sharply during the next several weeks. While these incidents were symptomatic of a deeper malaise, it is likely that the behavior of the Collinsville mob encouraged intolerance in neighboring communities.[32]

Rudolph Hofmeister also took note of this German-American experience.

> German-Americans did not easily forget what they suffered for their Teutonic background. This was expressed by Georg Seibel in his German Day speech of August 13,1933 when he summarized the persecution of Germans during World War I as follows: 'This pride in our Germanic origin has caused us German-Americans great suffering during the bitter war years. Thousands were interned, beaten, ruined in business because they were German. German books were burned, and 'patriotic' women avowed never to buy German goods again.

[31] Rudolph A. Hofmeister, *The Germans of Chicago*, (Champaign, Ill., Stipes Publishing Co., 1976), 113.
[32] Frederick Luebke, *The Bonds of Loyalty: German Americans and World War I*. (Northern Illinois University Press, 1974), 15.

We were called barbarians and Huns; we were the 'scum of humanity' because we were German. The world had gone mad with war hysteria.'[33]

With regard to the Chicago-based experience, Melvin G. Holli also analyzed this phenomenon, observing:

The wartime anti-German hysteria had been such a searing experience for Chicago Germans that much of their hitherto visible cultural presence vanished from public view. Although several scholars have pointed out that subcultures under oppression can survive hidden and virtually underground, that has rarely been the case in the United States. Here public celebration of ethnicity has been an important sustaining and reinforcing ritual. The larger-than-life prewar presence in the public life of Chicago almost vanished with no fraternal or political leaders to replace those who had been discredited by what Americanizers perceived to be disloyalty.[34]

The accusation of disloyalty and the need to meet in a basement must have seemed repugnant to these men. They were neither Nazi sympathizers nor criminals. Words they would use to describe themselves are: democratic, conservative, patriotic, Republicans, Catholic and anti-Communist. Their people were also fighting in Europe and the Pacific. But the reasons driving them underground were temporarily stronger than the lives they were living.

One of those reasons was that there had been another organization unfortunately associated with Germans in Chicago. La Vern J. Rippley reminds us that in the early 1930s

...under the leadership of Fritz Gissibl, German immigrants in Chicago organized a Sturm Abteilung (cell of storm troopers) incorporated as 'Teutonia' under the laws of the State of Illinois. This unit won the sanction of the German Nazi Party and eventually became the Nazi Party U.S.A.[35]

Thus the meeting in the Croat's basement was remarkable given the power of these collective memories, the anti-German *Zeitgeist*, and the perception of an FBI presence. In a time when the U.S. Treasury

---

[33] Rudolph Hofmeister, *The Germans of Chicago*, 79.
[34] Melvin G. Holli, et al. *Ethnic Chicago: A Multicultural Portrait.* (Grand Rapids, Mich., William B. Eerdmans Pub. Co., 1995), 107.
[35] La Vern J. Rippley, *The German Americans.* (University Press of America, 1984), 198.

Department was defining century-old German singing groups as pro-Nazi, the Schwobs can be forgiven their apprehensions.[36]

A measure of heroism is implied in this basement meeting when we realize that as the representatives of the combined 'social clubs' of Hungarian-German emigrés, nine clubs in all, it was therefore very likely, in their minds at least, that they were on some FBI surveillance roster.

In the thinking of these men, there was the crucial difference in *Weltanschauung* between their people and the Nazis. The racialism, imperialism and militarism of the Nazis was built upon ideas that were alien to the *Schwobs*. These men saw that the village-bound agricultural outlook of their old world was incompatible with the *Weltmacht* orientation of the Third Reich. They were positive that world conquest and a New Order were pretty far beyond the horizons of the *Donau-schwaben*. Convinced that ideological conflict had been imposed upon them from Hitler's Germany, these men believed that the Danube-Swabians, when left alone, were happy to buy land, to farm, go to church, hold festivals, raise children and to live off their labors in peaceful co-existence with other peoples. As Geza Paikert observed:

> However, it must be stressed that the kind-consciousness of these rural Swabians can best be assessed on the sociological rather than political plane. It contained little if any political element similar to that of the (Great) German folk or Volkstum; consequently, they had no demands to speak of in this respect. Their political 'awakening' came- as is almost a rule in similar instances- not from within and below, but from outside and above.
>
> The rural Swabians formed a closed society in their close-knit communities, which in a way resembled the ghetto in its narrowly parochial, rigidly observed norms and rules, which at once fortified and sterilized life in the village. This tight sociological unit was bound together by the cementing forces of common language, religion, culture and tradition, rather than political factors.[37]

These men were convinced, rightly or wrongly, that their people were really the *unverschuldete*. From their admittedly one-sided viewpoint, it wasn't the *Schwobs* that were making headlines on the front pages of the *Chicago Tribune*. The Chicago *Schwobs* therefore weren't

---

[36] Charles M. Barber, "Nordamerikanischer Sängerbund versus The U.S. Treasury Department, 1944-1946." *Yearbook of German-American Studies*, Vol.30, (1995).

[37] Geza Paikert, *The Danube Swabians*, 87-88.

as concerned with the victorious advance of the Yanks as they were with the coming of the Reds. Muth had given them a bitter foretaste of what was to come, information which must have been crushing to them. Five years later a group of Congressmen went on a field trip in Germany and Austria under the auspices of John J. McCloy. They confirmed in 1949 what the Chicago *Schwobs* were hearing from Kaspar Muth in 1944.

> The German expellees and refugees are individuals, single persons or in family groups, who have been expelled or have fled from several Eastern European countries and from the former German provinces placed under Polish administration, or from provinces occupied by the Soviet armies.
>
> Approximately 12,000,000 people were involved in this mass uprooting. They were herded across the borders without money or possessions into a war-ravaged country diminished in size by redrawn borders and divided into four zones of occupation, each under a different foreign rule. Over 8,500,000 of these expellees and refugees are scattered in western Germany comprising the American, British, and French zones of occupation and in the corresponding western zones of Austria, while allegedly 3,500,000 were sent into the Soviet zones of occupation in Germany and Austria.
>
> These 12,000,000 persons are considered Germans, either by birth or ancestry. The displaced persons who are under the protection of the International Refugee Organization are a distinctly different group of refugees, and they are not included in this figure.[38]

In fact, on the very day the *Deutsch-Ungarischer Hilfsverein* was organized there was a story that touched upon the Danube Germans in the *Chicago Tribune*. Ironically this story, like their catastrophe, remained in the back pages of the newspaper. It was in the form of one of the daily updates on the war from the Russian sectors, an aspect that could safely be relegated to the rear on September 17th, 1944.

The headline of this report said:

REDS ROLL THRU SOFIA ON ROAD TO YUGOSLAVIA

A map accompanied the article and encaptioned within that map were words that must have cut these men deeply. It said:

Romanian And Red Troops Only Ten Miles From Hungary

---

[38] *Expellees and Refugees of German Ethnic Origin*, Report # 1841, 81st Congress, 2nd Session, March 24,1950.

REDS ROLL THRU SOFIA ON ROAD TO YUGOSLAVIA

Begin Bridging Vistula Near Warsaw.

Along the Russian Front

(Story in adjoining column.)

TERRITORY TAKEN BY RUSSIANS

YESTERDAY'S REPORTED GAINS

GERMANS REPORT REDS ONLY 20 MILES FROM RIGA

RIGA

LATVIA

BAUSKA

DAUGAVPILS

LITHUANIA

MEMEL

KAUNAS

WILNO

EAST PRUSSIA

TILSIT

GROSNO

PINSK

BIALYSTOK

POLAND   RUSSIA

MODLIN

PRAGA

BREST-LITOVSK

WARSAW

RADOM

LUBLIN

REPORT REDS BRIDGE RIVER

KRAKOW

LWOW

ROMANIAN AND RED TROOPS ONLY 10 MILES FROM HUNGARY

LISKO

CZECHOSLOVAKIA

CERNAUTI

BUDAPEST

HUNGARY   VATRA-DORNEI

ORADEA   TRANSYLVANIA

CLUJ   BORSA

HUNGARIANS BATTLE ALLIES ON 50 MILE FRONT

ARAD   TARGU-MURES

LIPOVA

TIMISOARA

BRASOV

ROMANIA

PLOESTI

BELGRADE

YUGOSLAVIA

TURNU-SEVERIN

BUCHAREST

RUSSIAN TROOPS ENTER BULGARIAN CAPITAL

REASOTIA

VARNA

100 MILES

BULGARIA

BURGAS

SEPT. 17, 1944

SOFIA

Fighting sectors reported yesterday by Reds.

LONDON, Sept. 17 [Sunday]—(A.P.) Russian troops rolled thru the capitulated capital of Sofia yesterday, in their drive toward Yugoslavia, 30 miles beyond, while other soviet forces shelled burning Warsaw and began laying pontoon assault bridges across the Vistula river from the captured suburban area of Praga.

Berlin broadcasts reported, without confirmation, that three Red armies, using upward of 400,000 men, had begun a drive on Riga, Latvia, and that one spearhead in an 18 mile advance was only 20 miles south of the city on the Baltic sea.

A late dispatch said the Russians had begun stringing pontoons on the Vistula opposite Warsaw despite fire from German batteries. Moscow merely reported that the Russians had extended its artillery arc with the seizure of five more localities along the east bank of the river northwest of the Praga bridgehead.

Patriots Continue Fight.

A midnight Moscow bulletin said the Germans had used battalions of engineers and rear detachments, as well as Hungarian cavalry divisions in the fighting around Praga.

A bulletin from Gen. Bor, Polish underground leader in Warsaw, said his units had frustrated German efforts to establish strong points on the Vistula's western banks with which to meet the soviet onslaught.

In northern Transylvania, the Russians, aided by Romanian troops, captured more than 50 localities, Moscow said.

Reds Push Nearer Pass.

In northeastern Romania the Russians also captured Vatra-Dornei, 55 miles southeast of the tip of Czechoslovakia and only 10 miles from Hungarian-annexed Transylvania, in their advance thru the Carpathian mountains on the approaches to Bargau pass.

Budapest, Hungary, announced that Hungarian troops had collided with Russian or Romanian troops, or both, on a 50 mile front in western Romania, running between Lipova, Ineu and Beius. These localities are 25 to 38 miles from Hungary.

GERMAN WAR BULLETIN.

Germany's broadcast war report said yesterday:

"In south Transylvania German and Hungarian formations repulsed the enemy, who achieved an advance at Torenburg and on the Muresul.

"Several soviet attacks in the eastern Carpathians were repulsed. Soviet attempts to break thru launched with strong forces at Sanok and Krosno, were foiled. Twenty-seven soviet tanks were destroyed.

"Troops of the Waffen SS and Hungarian formations repulsed enemy forces northeast of Warsaw."

Chicago Tribune article, Sept. 17, 1944

What this signified to these men has to be understood within the context of the aftermath of World War I, especially the Treaty of Trianon, which by 1920 split their ancestral homeland into Hungary, Romania and Yugoslavia, dividing their people overnight. This meant that the Soviets were already deep in their beloved Banat, which had become western Romania. Therefore the headline was mistaken as far as they were concerned, for the Red Army was already in Hungary, in the villages and hamlets where their relatives were still living, in the land where many of them had been born. The Reds, like the Turks in 1738, were having their military revenge.

Compared to the horrendous things that were happening in their homeland, the fears and opposition of their club members meant as little to these men as the distress of the German butchers meant to the men of the German Aid Society of 1873. *Mitgefühl* compelled them to do something, in spite of the possibility of being labeled Nazi sympathizers or being arrested by the FBI for treasonous acts. They remembered that President Roosevelt had repeatedly stated that America wasn't at war with the German people. America was at war with Hitler and his Third Reich.

They reasoned that the President of the United States had thereby made it clear that he understood that the *kleine Leute* weren't really in control in Nazi Germany, and this gave them a rational justification for actions which really hinged upon their emotions. These terrible events were happening to grandmothers and grandfathers, fathers and mothers, brothers and sisters. Even so, they still couldn't force this issue into their own clubs.

They couldn't force the issue because of what their clubs meant to them. 'Club' may be placed solidly into one of the panels of the Hungarian-German social triptych in Chicago, right beside 'Church' and 'Family'. In this context the concept may be more usefully seen as 'village' rather than 'club'. The most important clubs were those built specifically around the town or village of origin in old Austria-Hungary, rather than some other kind of fraternal organization.

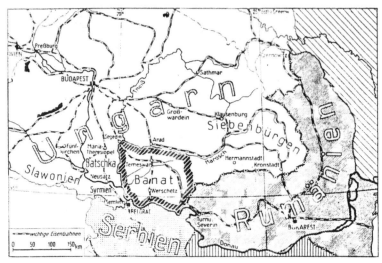

Entworfen von H. Schwalm.

25. Das Banat bei Ungarn bis 1918.

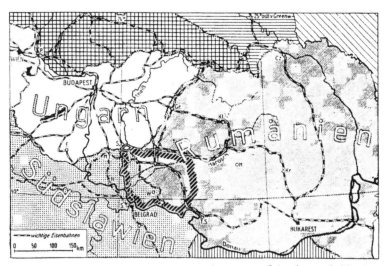

Entworfen von H. Schwalm.

26. Das Banat zwischen den Teilungsmächten seit 1919.

Source: *Handwörterbuch des Grenz und Auslanddeutschtum*, 208.

Maps showing the changed political relationship of the Banat after the Treaty of Trianon. Above: The Banat is completely in Hungary. Below: The Banat is divided.

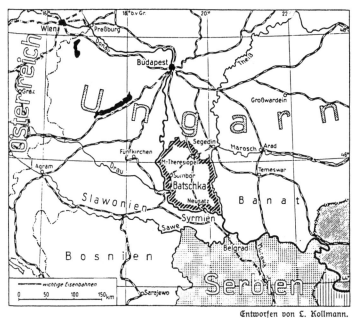

Entworfen von £. Kollmann.

46. Die Batſchka bei Ungarn bis 1918.

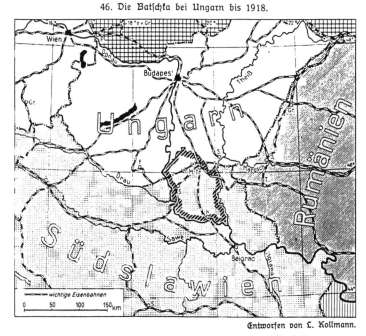

Entworfen von £. Kollmann.

47. Die Batſchka zwiſchen den Teilungsmächten ſeit 1919.

Source: *Handwörterbuch des Grenz und Auslanddeutschtum*, 292.

Maps on the prior page show the changed political relationship of the Batschka after the Treaty of Trianon. Top: The Batschka is completely in Hungary. Bottom: The Banat is divided.

At 'club' therefore, the members could enjoy *Gemütlichkeit,* engage in socio-economic networking, argue politics and, most importantly, teach their children the customs, traditions and wisdom of their forefathers *within their historic village group.* Club was therefore so much more than just a place to 'go' for the *Schwob.* It is better to say that club was a place to 'be'. It was because of this sanctuary-like function of their clubs that it was the last place in the world these men wanted to bring trouble to.

CHAPTER TWO

HELPLESS GESTURES

Even though these Swabian elders wouldn't consider bringing trouble into the inner sanctum of their club houses, they weren't the kind of men who could simply ignore the tragedy that was taking place. The man who must be primarily credited with arranging the first basement meeting of *Ungarndeutsche* leaders was a tailor by the name of Nick Pesch. Born in Jahrmark, Austria-Hungary, it is this man who was most determined to do something after the arrival of Kaspar Muth's letter. His commitment strengthened the others.

If the founders were at all hindered by memories of anti-German-ism, they could also have drawn strength from the history of German-American *Hilfswerk* (relief work). In that sense it is necessary to place the Chicago rescue operation within the tradition that had preceded it, as described by Luebke:

Each of the German churches participated extensively in the postwar relief work for Germany, where many thousands of persons faced malnutrition and starvation. Other German ethnic organizations also sprang into action in 1919, risking further nationalistic hostility. Attempts to help relatives and friends in Germany began immediately after the fighting ended. The armistice had not terminated the technical state of war, and the Allies, unreasonably fearful of Germany's recuperative powers, maintained their blockade of German ports until July 1919, when Germany ratified the Treaty of Versailles. Shortly after the ban on food shipments was lifted, ethnic leaders staged a massive rally in Philadelphia to mobilize German-American support for relief efforts. *Hilfswerk* committees, as they were called, were hastily established in cities wherever there were large numbers of Germans.
...They collected and dispatched packages of food and clothing, organized festivals and bazaars, staged concerts, and solicited gifts of money to support the program. Such activities were continued for five or six years until Germany regained a semblance of internal stability. Rarely, however, was the work coordinated. The *Vereins* and the churches preferred to work independently in

developing methods and goals of relief work and in deciding who in Germany would receive their aid.[39]

The Hungarian-Germans in Chicago especially 'preferred to work independently,' concentrating their efforts primarily on the needs of their people, needs which they were fully capable of meeting on the American scene. They had a vibrant, if somewhat encapsulated communal structure, forged even stronger during the Great Depression, framed within the Catholic faith and safely fenced in by socio-economic networking. The Chicago *Schwobs* possessed an economic engine capable of producing great pressure when needed. Their history had been one of insular existence, producing in them a self-sufficiency and frugality which served them well in America. *Schwobs* had always been land-hungry, and this mindset, combined with their old-world ways and work ethic, seems to have helped them achieve robust financial growth in Chicago. They invested heavily in businesses, apartment buildings, homes and land.

In 1925 three *Schwobs* bought prime lakefront property near the Wisconsin border in Lake Villa, Illinois, with the original purpose of building summer cottages. This idea was abandoned and in the summer of 1936 hundreds of Chicago's *Ungarndeutsche* came to the grand opening of the *German-Hungarian Old People's Home,* which was later to become the nucleus of the *German-Hungarian Aid Society* and the home base of the *Schwobs*. It was a fitting example of Swabian common sense, being both investment-wise and practically brilliant. They could escape the summer heat of the city to swim, fish and picnic in a beautiful setting of shade trees while their old folks looked on from the serenity of a large, screened-in porch. All the while they were holding valuable real estate under a non-profit tax status. This type of thinking was a reflection of values they had developed for over two centuries and had become a characteristic of the Chicago *Schwobs* as well.[40]

By 1940, as mentioned, the nine 'social clubs' of the *Donau-schwaben* had combined into an umbrella organization which solidified them while still allowing room for the unique competitiveness and separateness that these 'village-clubs' fostered. The *Schwobs* had their

---

[39] Luebke, *The Bonds of Loyalty*, 318.
[40] Richard Gunther, taped interview with author, 1996.

own insurance organization called the *Deutsch-Ungarisher Nationalitäten Kranken Unterstützungs Verein*, a form of Workmen's Compensation. They had their own Veteran's Aid and their own Youth Society. They patronized each other's businesses and attended each other's festivals and bazaars. They visited each other's clubs and commemorated events together. As a result they remained an airtight community, sealed by their long experience of outside hostility and harsh political realities. Economically speaking however, their charity work was only running the collective motor at idle speed. It was the coming of Dr. Muth's letter which changed things. Suddenly there was a desperate need to crank up the power because the engine finally had a real load to pull.

When Sam Baumann hurried out of Josef Maschek's barber shop that day in August 1944, he headed for a man who might be able to turn up the throttle on the *Donauschwaben* economic powerplant. He headed for the tailor shop on 3500 West North Avenue in Chicago where Nick Pesch made his meager living. By Swabian standards he was a poor man. He hadn't been featured as a speaker at the gala opening of the *Altenheim*, although Josef Maschek had. But this wasn't 1936, and many of the hundreds of German organizations Rudolph Hofmeister has noted had disappeared.[41] This was 1944 and now the President of the United Social Clubs of the Hungarian-Germans in Chicago was just a poor tailor.

Courtesy American Aid Society

Portrait of Nick Pesch which hangs in the A. A. S. Hall today.

Yet it is Nick Pesch, more than any other, who has been recognized by his people as being the leader of this rescue. The Chicago *Schwobs* laid a simple stone monument in the Lake Villa compound, which today serves as the Cultural Center of the Danube-Swabians and the Museum of the American Aid Society of German

---

[41] Hofmeister, *The Germans of Chicago*, p.113.

Descendants. It was done as a remembrance to the *Schwowe* who were killed after WW II. As a marker it was an unpretentious affair, just a stone on the ground and a wooden backboard with painted lettering, as shown below.

Photo: author

Original Danube Swabian Memorial, Lake Villa, Illinois

The inscription on the memorial reads:

NICK PESCH MEMORIAL
DIE LANDSMANNSCHAFT GEDENKET DEINER IN EHREN

IN MEMORY OF ALL OUR BELOVED PEOPLE, YOUNG AND OLD, WHO AFTER 1944 WERE ROBBED OF THEIR POSSES-SIONS, DEPRIVED OF THEIR GOD GIVEN RIGHTS AS HUMAN BEINGS AND PERISHED BY THE THOUSANDS OF HUNGER, COLD, AND DISEASE IN FIELDS AND CONCENTRATION CAMPS, THEIR ONLY CRIME BEING THAT THEY WERE GERMANS.

THIS MONUMENT HAS BEEN ERECTED BY THE AMERICAN
AID AND OLD PEOPLES HOME SOCIETY.
   TO ALL SURVIVORS WE SAY ONLY BY THE GRACE OF
GOD YOU AND I WERE SPARED.

ZUM GEDENKEN AN UNSERE LIEBEN LANDSLEUTE, DIE SEIT
1944 IHRER HABE UND IHRER MENSCHENRECHTE BERAUBT
WURDEN UND ZU TAUSENDEN AN HUNGER, KAELTE, UND
KRANKENHEITEN AUF FELDERN UND IN KONZENTRATIONS-
LAGERN UMKAMEN, NUR WEIL SIE DEUTSCHE WAREN.
   DIESES DENKMAL WURDE VON DER AMERICAN AID AND
OLD PEOPLES SOCIETY ERRICHTET.
DEN UEBERLEBENDEN RUFEN WIR ZU
AUCH DU WAEREST LAENGST IN DER RUH.
WENN NICHT DURCH GOTTES GNAD
DEIN LEBEN WAER BEWAHRT.

This memorial has now been redone in grand style and renamed the Nick
Pesch Memorial, offering him an opulence in death he never knew in
life.

Photo: author

Nick Pesch Memorial

Photo: author

Holding Mass at the Memorial, 1997. The man beside the priest is Joe Stein, Secretary of the American Aid Society of German Descendants and a survivor of Rudolphsgnad.

Photo: author

The *Schwobs* at Mass, Lake Villa, 1996.

It is interesting that this group of somewhat materialistically-oriented people awarded to one of the poorest among them the most authority. Moreover, Pesch was a rather unassuming man who really did not fit into the standard mold of a political leader. There are only two eyewitnesses left, at the time of this writing, who were present at the creation of the *Deutsch-Ungarischer Hilfsverein*, Richard Gunther and Helen Meiszner.

Gunther remembers Pesch in a way that differs markedly from the traditional leader-politician stereotype. He says:

Photo courtesy American Aid Society

Richard Gunther as he appeared at the beginning of the rescue.

Nick Pesch was a very mild-mannered, soft-spoken individual... he was one that could sooth the soul so to speak... wasn't good enough to be a preacher, but he was soft-spoken enough that you could not mistrust him...[42]

Pesch was beloved by the Chicago *Schwobs* even though he wasn't a role model in business. In fact, Richard Gunther remembers him as downright destitute because his small tailor shop just didn't 'do well'. Gunther says that Pesch had a wife and a daughter, but they never came around to any club activities, and therefore never figured at all in the extraordinary drama that the tailor with the nondescript clothes was living.

Much of Nick Pesch's life beyond the stage of the American Aid Society remains in the shadows, and there are hints of personal tragedy there as well. For our purposes here it is enough to know that the disaster overtaking his people moved this poor and quiet man and turned him into a fighter for them.

---

[42] Richard Gunther, taped interview. 1996.

Photo courtesy American Aid Society

Richard Gunther as a member of the Youth Group of the American Aid Societies

Photo courtesy American Aid Society

Riverview Park, Chicago. Helen Meiszner with her daughter, Joyce, during the rescue. (Standing on the float, in the rear). The float was for the German Day parade, circa 1952.

Photo courtesy Helen Meiszner

Richard Gunther and Helen Meizner, center of photo, circa 1956, with the quiet
heroines of the American Aid Societies, the women. Helen Meiszner has her
hand on the shoulder of Dr. Ludwig Leber of the *Caritasverband Für
Württemberg*. Leber was a pivotal figure in the European end of the relief work.

Gunther's remark about mistrust is important here and must be
explained. The *Schwobs* are a wary people, all the more so when anyone
comes asking for their hard-earned money. The 'village-mentality' we
have mentioned made them careful not to allow any other club to
aggrandize itself at their expense. Richard Gunther asserts that no
individual club president could have marshalled the efforts of the
Schwobs, and no loud and brassy man could have overcome the subtle
and hidden internecine 'village oneupmanship'. Pesch was apparently a
perfectly neutral candidate. It was obvious to all that he wasn't trying to
be a 'big man' because he was both quiet and poor. As we shall see,
however, when it came to his people and the trouble they were in, Nick
Pesch was like case-hardened metal, and his inner steel would prove
strong.

He would need the strength. What they were trying to do wasn't
going to be an easy task. This was activity that could be considered
legally dangerous in that winter of 1944-45. In 1936 the *Schwobs* had
marched down the main street in Lake Villa with all their flags flying

(alongside the Stars and Stripes). That kind of display was unthinkable now. After the Croatian basement meeting, where we may assume Dr. Muth's letter was read, it was still ten more months before the first general meeting of the *Deutsch-Ungarischer Hilfsverein* took place on July 31, 1945, at the Wicker Park Hall in Chicago, where Sam Baumann was apparently the janitor.

Photo courtesy American Aid Society

Founders of the American Aid Society.

Elections were held during this meeting and Pesch was elected as the President, making official the work he and others had been doing all along. Joseph Mueller was to become 1st Vice President. John Deppong, the Treasurer, a role particularly suited to the President of the *Deutsch-Ungarischer Nationalitäten Unterstützungs Verein*. Matthias Gartner went to the Finance Committee. John Funk accepted the role of *Archivar (archivist)*. Conrad Hack and Baumann went to the *Werbekommittee* (advertisement/public relations committee). John Kaiser and Christ Marshal were not yet seriously involved, but nevertheless important for the weight their names lent to the fledgling organization.

This was a meeting that underscored the difference ten months had made. The *Glogowatzer, Kerneir, Jahrmarker* and *Lieblinger* 'village clubs' had joined them, as had Chapters One and Two of the *Deutsch-Ungarisher Frauen Kranken Unterstützungs Verein.* This meant 78 new members had become involved. It was a significant start and quite a change from the Croatian basement.

At this meeting they had a guest speaker from the German American Congress for Democracy, William Schnell. This man had apparently only gotten out of Europe in 1941 and was therefore considered to be well acquainted with the situation there. Direct reporting was to become a characteristic of their meetings, especially later on, when this face-to-face contact helped to keep a sense of urgency alive. By the time of their second meeting on August 29, 1945, they were discussing writing a letter of thanks to the owner of the *Eintracht,* a popular German weekly for 'writing them up', and there was even a motion made to make the Wicker Park Hall their home. The German-Hungarian Aid Society was rooted, growing, and taking nourishment both from the German and the Danube-German collective body in spite of the hostile climate.[43]

Events proceeded at a steady pace. At the September 21st meeting it was reported that the *Deutsch-Ungarischer Frauen Verein* had joined, as well as the *St. Huberter* Club, adding 24 new members. By October 19th, three new members from St. Louis were added, along with the *Deutsch-Amerikanischer Unterstützung Verein.* By December 1945, the *Freidorfer* Club had come aboard.

While this Chicago activity was going on, things were happening at the highest levels of government. Enormous pressure began to be generated by a growing and well-financed Jewish lobby. Leonard Dinnerstein's methodically documented indictment of American anti-Semitism, *America and the Survivors of the Holocaust,* carefully records the exact nature of this process. In early July of 1945, Truman sent Earl G. Harrison, the former United States Commissioner of Immigration to investigate incredible allegations of mistreatment of Jewish concentration camp survivors. Dinnerstein wrote:

---

[43] Official minutes of the *Deutsch-Ungarischer Hilfsverein,* July-August 1945, presently located at the Cultural Center of the Danube Swabians, Lake Villa, Illinois.

The Harrison Report hit the leaders at the highest level in Washington like a bombshell and led to a scurry of activity for change. At the outset no one would have believed that the findings of the investigators would be as devastating as they turned out. But Harrison and his entourage uncovered conditions within the DP camps that only the most heartless and indifferent bureaucrat could have ignored. In fact, none of the responsible political and military officials who read about them failed to implement changes. Ultimately, the Harrison report affected American diplomatic relations with Great Britain and led to the movement for ameliorative legislation by Congress.[44]

In spite of criticism about him, such as is found in Susan Hartmann's *Truman and the 80th Congress*,[45] it is only fair to point out that he did send Earl Harrison to investigate the situation and then issued his famous directive on December 22, 1945, which declared:

The grave dislocation of populations in Europe resulting from the war has produced human suffering that the people of the United States cannot and will not ignore. This Government should take every possible measure to facilitate full immigration to the United States under existing quota laws.

...Visas should be distributed fairly among persons of all faiths, creeds and nationalities. I desire that special attention be devoted to orphaned children to whom it is hoped the majority of visas will be issued.[46]

Interestingly, there is no mention of Truman's statement in the minutes of the *Deutsch-Ungarischer Hilfsverein* (DUHV), but it did represent an encouraging sign that the problem of Europe's Displaced millions was being considered by the President. In January 1946, District 572 of the Greater Beneficial Union of Pittsburgh had joined and both the Catholic Welfare Association and the American Friends Service Committee had promised its aid. Other indices of organizational health also began appearing in the minutes. Pesch was charged with getting them a charter. In February they needed a checking account and were talking about a banquet. By March 1946, they had a hefty $651.00 in their account. The motor was running.[47]

---

[44] Leonard Dinnerstein, *America and the Survivors of the Holocaust*. (New York: Columbia University Press, 1982), 39.

[45] Susan M. Hartmann, *Truman and the 80th Congress*. (Columbia: University of Missouri Press, 1971).

[46] Directive by President Harry S. Truman, December 22, 1945.

[47] Various minutes of the DUHV. American Aid Society Records, Danube Swabian Cultural Center, Lake Villa, Illinois.

Source: American Aid Societies Monthly Reporter, Vol.1, No.3, Philadelphia, Pa. June 1948.

People waiting for aid at the *Christlichen Hilfswerk*
in the main train station in Salzburg, Austria.

Photo courtesy Helen Meiszner

Goods collected for shipment to Europe, November 1948. The woman
on the right, standing at the crate, is holding the minutes of the DUHV.

Pesch presided over the work of convincing other clubs and organizations while the rest of the members did the physical work of collecting food and clothing donations, buying CARE packages, organizing banquets, having bunco parties, bazaars, and raffling off prizes. In fact, for the life of the organization (as is still true in the present), festivals and banquets and celebrations consumed much of the energy of the rank and file members, and they were good at it. Tons of material relief would be collected, packaged and mailed, but the real mission of Nick Pesch, and the pivotal figures who would gather around him, had yet to be enunciated in a clear, unmistakable voice.

One by one, certain exceptional individuals would come forward from among the membership to help define and further the work of rescue. Matt Bastion for example, a man who had begun his own hair products company, donated one thousand bottles of his Four Penny Shampoo to the cause. Eventually he allowed his factory on 1220 North Bosworth in Chicago to become a home for their meetings, then someplace to store the huge amount of clothing and foodstuffs they were collecting, and finally their first real corporate address.

A young Richard Gunther stepped up with his infectiously bright personality and his musical abilities, initially to make some spending money by playing music for the DUHV after their meetings. He became committed to their work and thereby brought the younger crowd with him.[48] Sam Baumann, a man full of love for his *Landsleute*, donated the energy of an indefatigable and indispensable worker.

Whenever the members would become discouraged over the exhausting work facing them, all of which was over and above their normal routines, or would become embroiled in overheated arguments, a man named Peter Paul Reiner would raise his arms dramatically in the air like some Swabian Moses and remind everyone of their real mission by shouting at the top of his voice, over and over again:

"Wir müsse die landsleute heeeeeeeeeelllllllfe!"[49]

---

[48] Richard Gunther, taped interview, May 1996.
[49] Ibid, taped interview, May 1996.

And then there was Helen Meiszner's step-father, Math Gatsch, himself deeply dedicated to this cause, who made the propitious suggestion that they enlist the aid of his new son-in-law, John C. Meiszner.[50]

---

[50] Helen Meiszner, taped interview, April 1997.

CHAPTER THREE

THE AMERICAN SCHWOB

The Chicago rescue depended on certain individuals who became committed to this cause and then worked with such energy and passion that they were able to help overcome the natural inertia of people who are secure and safe, urging them to give their time and money. This probably couldn't have been done by individual effort alone. Along with the impact of information from Dr. Kaspar Muth in Rumania, there were other forces at work on the Chicago *Schwobs*, especially their Catholic clergymen, who were adept at pushing them with the kinetic energy of language. Consider these words by Monsignor Edward E. Swanstrom, the Executive Director of the War Relief Services Division of the National Catholic Welfare Conference:

> In the fall of 1945 I went through Germany and Austria and saw the arrival of the deportation trains filled with expellees. These trains were sent off into the night with their hopeless, and despoiled human cargo without destination and without any supplies for the journey. Mostly these trains were collections of cattle cars which were securely locked so that the people could not escape on the way. I saw these cattle cars opened, and I saw the faces of the bewildered men and women and little children as they staggered out into a bombed station and looked around them into nothingness."[51]

The Chicago *Schwobs* were able to generate their own momentum in the economic and social sphere, but without any propulsion from the arena of *American* politics, they could not have carried off their rescue. Fortunately they had such a force and were willing to use it.

The first time John C. Meiszner's name appears in the minutes of the *Deutsch-Ungarischer Hilfsverein* is March 15, 1946, one month before their first banquet. At that time he was an aggressive and

---

[51] *The Expellees and Surplus Population*, speech delivered by Edward E. Swanstrom, Executive Director, War Relief Services, National Catholic Welfare Conference, Sunday, Dec.10,1950. A.A.S. Banquet, Chicago, Illinois.

successful young businessman, a funeral home owner since 1936, who was broadening his business base by prolific club and political activity. Rudolph Hofmeister observed in his book *The Germans of Chicago:*

> The Germans seem to be fond of organizing clubs, if one may believe John Meiszner, past President of the Germania Club and member of forty-two others, who stated in an interview in the Sun Times Sunday edition of August 18,1968: "Put three Germans together and in five minutes you'll have four clubs."[52]

Photo courtesy Helen Meiszner

John C. Meiszner in his favorite role

Math Gatsch knew that his new son-in-law had a prospering business and some 'friends'. Maybe he could help them with their banquet. Through Helen Meiszner he was approached about it and he agreed to help.

If Nick Pesch epitomized the quiet and stoic Swabian elder, born in the old country, outwardly humble and speaking English badly, then John Meiszner was the exact opposite. He was the Americanized *Schwob*, Chicago-born and articulate in English, he was stylish, hoarding 'connections' and talking to the 'big men' of the Chicago *Obrigkeit* as one of their equals. He was charismatic and carried himself with confidence and the effect he had on the DUHV seems to have been immediate.[53]

At the April monthly meeting Christ Marshall reported that the banquet had been a success, showing a profit of $1,138.74. Whether Meiszner's influence helped is unclear, but by the meeting in May there were distinct impressions of his presence. Bold new ideas begin to appear in the minutes. The most startling one suggested something incredible.

---

[52] Hofmeister, *The Germans of Chicago*, 116.
[53] Taped interviews with Helen Meiszner and Richard Gunther.

> Motion made and seconded that five men be sent to Detroit as a committee to get all information about bringing people to Canada. The Consulate should be contacted to find out whether people are able to come in from the camps in Yugoslavia...
>
> Mr. Andrew Boettinger offered to 'get up a letter that can be sent to the Senators.'[54]

There is a noticeable difference from the minutes of their earlier meetings, especially Pesch's handling of a letter to the State Department

Photo courtesy Helen Meiszner

John Meiszner speaking on December 10, 1950, at the Annual Banquet of the American Aid Societies in the Logan Square Masonic Temple.

asking for permission to send used clothes to Europe. The answer they received was apparently so complex that Pesch sent it to someone for clarification. Whereas the focus before Meiszner's appearance was on sending relief out, after his debut it was centered on bringing people in.

It just appears that after John Meiszner's arrival things began to be different. In fact, the very next month there was a dramatic change in the

---

[54] DUHV Minutes, Protokall #11, May 17,1946.

flavor of their meetings. For the next eighteen months, from April, 1946 until September 1947, the minutes would take on an Americanized format by being written exclusively in English. In June Meiszner was appointed the Director of the Youth Organization, an enormously important position within the Swabian environment. By July, four months after his entrance onto the scene, the organization's name had changed. Henceforth they would call themselves the *American* German-Hungarian Aid Society (until April 27,1948, when they would become the American Aid Societies, Chicago Chapter.) The 'American *Schwob*' had appeared on the scene and his voice was as strong and confident as America itself.

Photo courtesy Helen Meiszner

John Meiszner at the dedication of the
Lake Villa Memorial to Swabian war-dead.

By now the rescue work had taken on impressive proportions. In September 1946, it was reported that 138 clothing packages had been sent to Saalfelden, Salzburg, Austria at a postage cost of $197.38. They were positive that 50 CARE packages could be sent each month and they had a check for $750.00 waiting until the paperwork could be completed.

Meiszner reported that the car raffle was going well. They had $422.50 toward this purchase already and he was able to announce that he had secured the co-operation of the *Chicago Herald American* in getting 'stars' for the November 6th rally they were planning. By October they had $865.00 towards the car and they were going to have a 'Sports Celebrity Night' at the November rally.

Also in October the 'Chicago Formula' seemed to have been adopted among the *Schwobs* of New York. Officially founded in October 1946, as the *Amerikanischer Deutsch-Ungarischer Hilfsverein*, they soon changed their name to the American Banater Relief Society of New York, Inc. Although they remained independent, it is apparent that they mimicked the Chicago style. The Pesch-Meiszner dynamism had affected other Hungarian-German groups.

All of this work was taking place in a clear context of anti-Germanism. In December 1946, the constitution of the International Refugee Organization was approved by the United Nations. The IRO was created to take over for the United Nations Relief and Rehabilitation Administration (UNRRA) which was the official agency charged with the tasks of maintenance, repatriation and resettlement of the displaced persons of Europe.

Photo courtesy Helen Meiszner

Swabian women packing clothes for shipment to Europe.

In the section of the constitution of the IRO which dealt with defining who was eligible for IRO help, the *Schwobs* learned of the IRO 'exclusion clause'. The constitution stated that:

> ...the foregoing definitions are subject to certain exclusions, as follows:
> 4. Persons of German ethnic origin, whether German nationals or members of German minorities in other countries, who-
> (a) have been or may be transferred to Germany from other countries;
> (b) have been, during the Second World War, evacuated from Germany to other countries;
> (c) have fled from, or into, Germany, or from their places of residence into countries other than Germany, to avoid falling into the hands of the Allied armies.[55]

This 'exclusion clause' neatly walled the *Donauschwaben* out. In the face of such obstacles it was only natural for them to turn to John Meiszner and his clean-cut American audaciousness and Made-In-The USA charisma. He was the best 'politically connected' man the *Schwobs* of Chicago had. And John Meiszner had family trapped in Tito's Yugoslavia.

Helen Meiszner testifies that one of the main reasons Meiszner had such a bold attitude was that he had figured out an ingenious angle to further 'political friendships' with the aid of his funeral business. It is a study in Swabian business sense. Many politicians at that time preferred to travel in ostentatious limousines, the more noticeable the better. John Meiszner had long black Cadillac limos which he used in his funerals.

---

[55] *Expellees and Refugees of German Ethnic Origin*, Report of a Special Subcommittee of the Committee on the Judiciary, House of Representatives, Report #1841, March 24,1950. p.20. The term Allied armies in (c) refers primarily to Soviet and Yugoslav partisan forces.

Photo courtesy Helen Meiszner

The Political Schwob. Above: John Meiszner on the Hunter For Mayor Committee (Chicago, Republican). Below: John Meiszner and Joseph Martin, Republican Minority Leader of the House of Representatives. Notice the Chicago city sticker on Meiszner's Cadillac and the 'Official Joseph Martin Car' placard.

Photo courtesy Helen Meiszner

The simple expedient of taping a placard on these cars transformed them from one purpose to the next, enabling him to charge up political credits by providing chauffeured limo service to politicians he was 'working for'. To be whisked away from the airport and motored around town was a service that rated high with politicians, especially those still struggling. Perhaps this is how John Meiszner learned and exploited the fundamental truth that lawmakers are just men, after all, and that laws are sometimes just as transitory and fragile as their creators.

CHAPTER FOUR

A FOOT IN THE DOOR

America and the Survivors of the Holocaust, by Leonard Dinnerstein, contains a fascinating study of the forces which by the end of 1946 had begun to make the problem of the displaced persons in Europe a major issue.[56] The light that the Harrison Report was able to shine into the ugly realities of anti-Semitism still in effect in the DP camps drove many to support the cause of relief for the DP's in the form of immigration legislation. *Life* magazine declared on September 23, 1946, that:

> ...the most shocking fact about the plight of these displaced persons is not that they are interned. It is the fact that the United States Government and people have the means to open the door for many of them but have not done so.[57]

Articles would eventually appear all over the country in favor of efforts on behalf of the displaced people of Europe. Stalwarts such as *The Saturday Evening Post*, *The New York Times*, *The Washington Post* and *The Los Angeles Daily News* would be among the many that indicated their support. Dinnerstein reveals how this came about through the work of the most effective political-action group, the Citizen's Committee on Displaced Persons (CCDP). This group was the brainchild of Lessing Rosenwald, president of the American Council for Judaism. Dinnerstein writes:

> The most important meeting occurred at a luncheon of an AJC [American Jewish Committee] subcommittee in early November [1946] where the groundwork and strategy for the entire campaign emerged. The conferees agreed with Rosenwald's idea that a broadly based national citizen's committee, composed of prominent Christian, and perhaps a few Jewish, leaders from the ranks of the ministry, business, labor, education, and social welfare should be formed. It would serve as a "political action and propaganda group which could ...swing public sentiment in favor of relaxing immigration

---

[56] Leonard Dinnerstein, *America and the Survivors of the Holocaust*, pps.117-182.
[57] *Life* Magazine, September 23, 1946.

laws in order to admit a fair share of displaced persons in this country." Thus, in the classic tradition of lobbying, a narrow humanitarian interest (aiding Jewish DP's) would take on an expanded focus (helping all DP's, 80 percent of whom were Christian), and would strive for widespread support.[58]

Truman's State of the Union Message on January 6, 1947, reflected that 'widespread support' and the pressure he had been under since the Harrison Report had been published. The United States, he said:

> ...can be proud of its part in caring for peoples reduced to want by the ravages of war, and in aiding nations to restore their national economies. We have shipped more supplies to the hungry peoples of the world since the end of the war than all other countries combined.
>
> However, so far as admitting displaced persons is concerned, I do not feel that the United States has done its part. Only about 5,000 of them have entered this country since May 1946. The fact is that the executive agencies are now doing all that is reasonably possible under the limitation of existing law and established quotas. Congressional assistance in the form of new legislation is needed. I urge the Congress to turn its attention to this world problem in an effort to find ways whereby we can fulfill our responsibilities to these thousands of homeless and suffering refugees of all faiths.[59]

Truman's words may have seemed comforting to those interested in helping the DP's, but for the *Schwobs* of Chicago however, the other side of the argument was always as close at hand as their daily newspaper.

> The Veterans of Foreign Wars, the American Legion, and other groups with like views presented a solid front of opposition to plans for immigration, and their position was reflected editorially in *The Chicago Tribune*.[60]

But immigration legislation had much bigger foes than the nativists represented by the American Legion, which would do an about-face after visiting the DP camps anyway. Dinnerstein argues that in the Senate and the House there was much hidden anti-Semitism, which was reinforced by the general impression that most of the DP's were Jews and Communists, which was completely false. The CCDP apparently had great difficulty in even finding a legislator to introduce its proposed bill.

---

[58] Dinnerstein, *America and the Survivors of the Holocaust*, 122.

[59] *Memo to America: The DP Story, The Final Report of the Displaced Persons Commission*, (Washington, D.C.: Government Printing Office, 1952), 11.

[60] Ibid, 11.

Finally, having waited for strategic reasons until the Senate approved the Constitution of the IRO, the CCDP went to

> ...the House of Representatives where they had to make do with William G. Stratton, Representative-at-Large from Illinois. A later in-house AJC memo indicated that "Mr. Stratton would not have been our choice." Efforts were made to find a Judiciary Committee member, but "the feeling was so adverse at the time no one cared to 'stick his neck out' by introducing such a bill."[61]

Introduced on April 1, 1947, the Stratton Bill called for the admission of 100,000 persons a year for a period of 4 years under the watchful eyes of the Departments of State and Justice. For the most part the major newspapers came out in support of the measure. The House Judiciary Committee under the chairmanship of Frank Fellows of Maine began hearings on the bill two weeks later. The CCDP carefully selected its witnesses, including only two Jews by design. Truman sent an impressive array of witnesses to testify for the measure, notably the Secretary of State, George C. Marshall, the Secretary of War, Robert W. Patterson, and the Attorney General, Tom Clark. Support came from the pulpits as well.

> Church groups such as the Federal Council of Churches of Christ in America and the National Catholic Welfare Conference and smaller affiliates, indicated not only their whole-hearted support, but also indicated a willingness to assist in the actual resettling of the immigrants in the United States.[62]

It was in this atmosphere of political possibilities that Pesch and Meiszner finished laying the foundation of their 'national organization' by holding a conference at the Morrison Hotel in Chicago. By the time of their first 'national convention' on July 5-6, 1947, in Cleveland, it becomes even more evident that the Hungarian-German groups in other cities decided to defer to Pesch and Meiszner's leadership. By the time of the publication of their first 'official' bulletin, *'The Monthly Reporter'* in April 1948, the cloning process may be said to have been fairly complete when the New York group announced it had purchased a *'nagelneue 1948 Nash Sedan'* for a raffle. Meiszner had personally run the Chicago raffle and had turned in a tidy $2,139.99 profit by December 1946.[63]

---

[61] Dinnerstein, *America and the Survivors of the Holocaust*, 131-32.

[62] *Memo to America: The DP Story*, 14.

[63] *Monthly Reporter*, April 1948, Vol.1, No 1., 3.

On June 24th, 1947, Pesch and Meiszner were 'elected' as delegates to the July convention of the *American Aid Societies for the Needy and Displaced Persons of Central and Southeastern Europe* in Cleveland. At the next monthly meeting Pesch offered his resignation to the Chicago *Schwobs*. He had been elected President of the National Organization. John Meiszner had become the National Secretary. Chicago had won the battle over where the seat of the organization should be as well as where the Charter would be taken out. The parliamentary action at this convention was essentially a *tour de force* for Pesch and Meiszner.

Richard Gunther and Helen Meiszner both testify that this 'national phase' was initiated by advice received from Washington D.C. through John Meiszner. It is probable that this came from Senator William Langer of North Dakota. The 'advice' was that they needed a 'national' organization if they wanted to attract any attention on Capitol Hill. In fact, letters from Langer were being discussed as early as May 27, 1947.[64] In August 1947, a letter from Langer was read which explained the legal meaning of the term 'Displaced Person' to the *Schwobs*.[65]

From here on, Pesch and Meiszner focused primarily on the same political tactics that everyone else was using. While the ordinary relief work went on among the rank and file, the critical work of consolidation, of becoming a unified political presence had really just begun. They were advised to do the grunt work of lobbying the old fashioned way, sending telegrams, gathering petitions, writing letters, adopting resolutions, and sending delegations to Washington. They were an indefatigable pair. In May of 1948, they went to Capitol Hill to lobby in person, even though, as Richard Gunther testifies, Meiszner had to pay Pesch's train fare. But then, how could the National Secretary appear without the National President?

By this stage they had each written hundreds of letters and telegrams, missives in which there could be detected a growing sense of authority. They had become a 'national' force, if only in their own eyes.

---

[64] DUHV Minutes, Protokal #23, May 27, 1947, Danube Swabian Cultural Center, Lake Villa, Illinois.
[65] DUHV Minutes, Protokal #26, August 26, 1947, Danube Swabian Cultural Center, Lake Villa, Illinois.

Up to this point the focus had been on getting other organizations to join with them. Now they recognized the need to attach themselves to more powerful institutions. The preference for 'working independently' had to go the way of their ethnically-oriented name and be abandoned on the American political scene. In the very first *'Monthly Reporter'*, co-editor Peter Yanker explained to the readers why they had allied themselves with the newly formed National Catholic Resettlement Council, a sub-division of the War Relief Services Division of the powerhouse National Catholic Welfare Conference:

> The most important problem that stands before the American Aid Society is the problem of resettlement of the Donauschwaben... The people descending from the Donauschwaben represent only a very small percentage of the total population of the United States. Also, we are not concentrated in any one territory to exert any political or moral influence effective enough to bring about the immigration of these people to the United States or any other country. In view of all that, it is out of necessity that we should work with a more powerful and influential group. Since the Catholic Resettlement Council is such a group and has the problem of the Donauschwaben at heart it is only natural that we should work with them to achieve our objectives.[66]

This first publication, (which incidentally beat Chicago to the punch), was a collaborative effort of the *American-German-Hungarian Relief Society of Philadelphia* and the *American Banater Relief Society of Buffalo, New York and Vicinity*. It seemed to encapsulate the Pesch-Meiszner formula, especially in the explanation given for the name changes. By November 1948, this practical advice was dominant. All of the eleven Chapters (except Mansfield, Ohio) had 'American' preceding their name.

By November 1948, the Chicago National Office had taken over the *Monthly Reporter*. First to go was the impractical 8½ x 12½ format. The National Office immediately adopted the standard 8½ x 11 paper size. Next went the quaint title and the drab appearance. The word *American* became prominent and a masthead drawing, capturing the most urgent and noble qualities of relief work was added. The newsletter immediately took on a more professional, polished look. Not surprisingly, John Meiszner's name appeared front and center in a

---

[66] *Monthly Reporter*, April 1948, Vol.1, No.1., 3. American Aid Society Records, Danube Swabian Cultural Center, Lake Villa, Illinois.

column called *From The Desk Of The Secretary*, and Nick Pesch had a column beside his. The 'National Office' had assumed control.

The *Schwobs* were also being guided in their political efforts by Monsignor Swanstrom, who, from his position as the Executive Director of the War Relief Services Division of the NCWC kept close watches in the halls of Congress and knew exactly when it was time to apply persuasion to key legislators. But the Catholic lobby would not be enough. They needed a politician.

When Senator Homer Ferguson of Michigan and eight of his fellow Senators introduced a Senate version of the Stratton Bill, the Schwobs got their first big break. It was during the Senate Judiciary Committee hearings that the composition of the committee left a Republican Senator from North Dakota with the crucial 'swing vote' on close decisions. Dinnerstein observes:

> Senator Langer, of German ancestry, represented a state where the German-Russians (Germans who had settled in Russia in the early nineteenth century but who had retained their native culture) counted as the leading ethnic group. Langer had started his political career in the German areas of central and southwestern North Dakota, and those counties supported him heavily at the polls. He had great affinity with the German people and according to two Washington reporters, Robert S. Allen and William V. Shannon, his pro-German proclivities during the early 1940's had "strong Nazi and anti-Semitic overtones." A staff member of the Senate Judiciary Committee later recalled the North Dakotan as being "almost pro-Nazi." Despite these allegations Langer fit no prescribed label and had, in fact, engaged in activities which suggested generous humanitarian instincts. In 1947 and 1948 he favored broad social welfare programs to aid the underprivileged in the United States and in October 1945, the North Dakota senator had written to President Truman indicating that he "felt very strongly that we are repudiating the very principles for which we fought when we do not insist that the Jews be allowed admittance to Palestine." He had also indicated in a public meeting in Beulah, North Dakota, on November 9, 1947, that he planned to vote for the Stratton bill. Therefore the CCDP assumed that he would be with them in the Judiciary Committee deliberations.
>
> But the CCDP guessed wrong. Langer would support DP legislation only if the Senate Judiciary Committee incorporated his proposal to include the *Volksdeutsche* among the beneficiaries of the proposed measure.[67]

---

[67] Dinnerstein, *America and the Survivors*, 165.

By the end of the legislative battling the *Volksdeutsche* had been included with the rest of the DPs. The *Monthly Reporter* of June 1948, was privileged to announce under the heading '*Welcome News*' that

> On Friday, June 18,1948, the House of Representatives adopted the final version of the Displaced Persons Bill. There is no doubt that the Senate will pass the measure also...
>
> ...In other words, 27,000 of our people will be able to enter over the next two years. If we consider the fact that there are over 200,000 persons of German origin from Czechoslovakia, Romania and Yugoslavia in Austria alone, and if we add about 200,000 who are in Germany, it means that about 5 to 5.5 percent of our people will be able to find a new home in this country. Nevertheless, even this meagre achievement represents a victory for the American Aid Societies. Without our delegations in Washington, without our petitions, resolutions and telegrams, even this achievement would have been impossible...
>
> ...A great deal of credit for this achievement is due Senator William N. Langer who steered the original amendments through the Senate and Congressmen Kersten and Youngblood who made the same efforts in the House.[68]

The battle had indeed been long and bitter, and the pressure brought to bear on the lawmakers from all sides was tremendous, especially from proponents of a DP Act.

> Opponents of the legislation repeatedly referred to the so-called pressure groups at work for this legislation, with particular emphasis on the Citizens Committee for Displaced Persons- both by allusion and by name- and on its force of registered lobbyists. Those opposed to favorable action seemed to resent this group.[69]

On June 25th, 1948, the President signed Public Law 774, The Displaced Persons Act. The *Schwobs* now had a foot in the tight-fitting door of U.S. immigration policy. This was a historic first. Not only had the U.S. Government temporarily pulled open barricades to immigration, but it had also created an agency, The Displaced Persons Commission, specifically empowered and funded to see that the goals of Public Law 774 were achieved.

---

[68] *Monthly Reporter*, June 1948, Vol.1, No.3, 3. A.A.S. Records, Danube Swabian Cultural Center, Lake Villa, Illinois.

[69] *Memo to America: The DP Story*, 26.

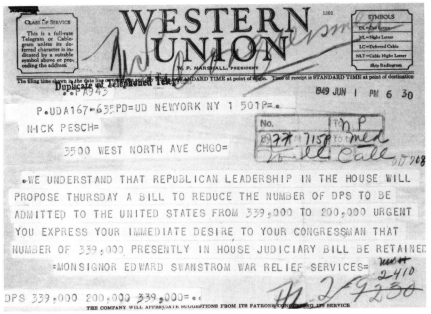

Source: American Aid Society

Typical telegram sent to Nick Pesch in the heat
of legislative fighting by Monsignor Swanstrom.

For the *Donauschwaben* there was an even more important aspect
to the creation of the Displaced Persons Commission. This was the
appointment of Edward Mark O'Connor as one of the three
Commissioners. The significance of this appointment was that O'Connor
had been the Executive Assistant to War Relief Services, National
Catholic Welfare Conference, since 1943. The *Schwobs* therefore had a
most sympathetic ear on the very agency charged with resettling refugees
in the U.S. This was to play a key role in the battles that were still to
come for them. Everyone concerned saw the problems coming, most of
all Truman. He joined a chorus of voices in publicly castigating the bill
even as he signed it into law.

> In a statement concerning the bill, the President declared that the bill as passed
> by Congress consisted of a combination of the worst features of both the Senate
> and the House bills. He maintained that elements of the bill '...form a pattern

of discrimination and intolerance wholly inconsistent with the American sense of justice.'[70]

It is interesting to remember here that it was the very next day, June 26, 1948, that the Allies would begin air-lifting supplies into the blockaded city of Berlin. In German this is called the *Berliner Luft Brücke* (Air Bridge), an event which touched the German people deeply. We may assume it affected the *Donauschwaben* as well.

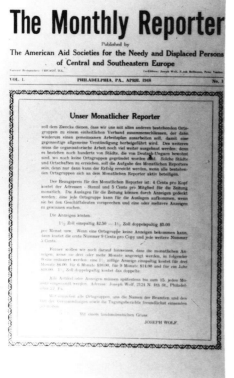

Courtesy American Aid Society

First publication of the American
Aid Societies, April 1948

Courtesy American Aid Society

American Aid Society Bulletin,
December, 1948

The difference in design that Chicago made is evident above.

---

[70] Ibid, 27.

AMERICAN AID SOCIETIES

BETRACHTUNGEN —

ung. Laut Gesetz koennen unsere Leute einwandern, das heisst, wenn sie den Anforderungen der Gesetze genuege leisten, und ihre Affidavits, ihre finanzielle Guarantie wie auch Ueberfahrt gesichert haben.

Dadurch, dass so viele Fluechtlinge keine Bekannte oder Verwandte hier haben, erschwert das ihre Sache ausserordentlich. Aber auch solche, die Verwandte hier haben, sind oft verhindert heruober zu kommen, weil es den Verwandten am noetigen Gelde fehlt.

die engeren Verwandten in Europa, manchmal 20 bis 30 personen, herueber kommen zu lassen. Die Hillsvoreine muessen versuchen da Abhilfe zu leisten. Die angesammelten Umsiedlungsfonds sollten daluer die Antwort sein.

Andere Probleme: Die Verteilung von den Liebesgaben an die Notleidenden in Europa ist in schlimmster Unordnung. Gewiss, es wurden bei Konventionen Beschluesse gefasst, die Verteilung zu organisieren, aber es fehlt die Einsicht bei den Mitgliedern, dass eine geordnete Verteilung das Beste ist. So lange jede Ortsgruppe tut was sie will und sich um die Beschluesse der Konventionen nicht kuemmert, wird der Chaos weiter bestehen und die Leute in Europa der Verzweiflung nahe gebracht.

Eines ist gewiss, das Problem ist zu gross, um einigermassen zufriedenstellend geloest zu werden. Aber als Anfang, um irgend ein Problem zu loesen—ganz egal, ob gross oder klein—muss Verstaendniss und guter Wille vorhanden sein

Wenn die Direktorensitzung in Cincinnati am 21. November eine zufriedenstellende Loesung fuer all diese Probleme findet, dann gebuehrt ihr groesste Anerkennung.

Nick Pesch.

COME ONE!! COME ALL!!

Let us make this one affair, that will long be remembered by all the friends and members of the Chicago chapter of the American Aid Society.

THE COMMITTEE.

Edward Mark O'Connor, Executive Assistant to War Relief Services NCWC, who has just been appointed to the Displaced Persons Commission by President Truman. Mr. O'Connor, who is a graduate of Notre Dame University, has been with War Relief Services NCWC since August 1943.

ZUR BEACHTUNG!

Chicago Mitglieder. Unsere Kanzlei ist abends geschlossen. Mittwoch Abend Geschaeftsstunden, jedoch **nur** bei vorheriger Verabredung. Telefonieren sie BRunswick 8-7268 und fragen sie nach Frau Simak.

BANQUET —

rope to help relieve them in their suffering and need.

To see and hear Senator William Langer-of North Dakota is worth the price of admission of $2.50 alone, but the Chicago chapter is furnishing a Dinner — Entertainment and Dancing in the evening—in conjunction with this.

CHRISTMAS FUND

Make your contributions for Christmas, Well Wishers and Greetings, will be published in our next edition.

COME ONE COME ALL to the LOGAN SQUARE MASONIC TEMPLE, December 12, 1948 to enjoy good food—refreshmentsand hear a great man like Senator Langer speak, and last but not least to help your needy and displaced friends over seas. Halls open at 3:30 p.m. Program starts at 5 p.m.

Verwandten Suchdienst!

Josef MARTIN, geb. 1886 oder 1888 in Nagy Forak, wird gesucht von John Prem.

Adam VALENDA, geb. in Cervenka, ungefaehr 52-58 Jahre alt Gesucht von Michael Jung.

Jacob BURGER und Frau Elizabeth, geb. Schaeler von Sekitsch. Gesucht von den Neffen Nikolaus Schaefer.

Stefan STIKL und Frau Kristine, sowie Josef WELKER. Gesucht von Frau Zelestine Vollmannshauser aur Pancsowa, Startcowa, Jugoslawien.

Wer Auskunft erteilen kann, wende sich bitte an die Kanzlei der American Aid Societies.

Only 50c for one year.

SUBSCRIPTION BLANK FOR
AMERICAN AID SOCIETIES BULLETIN
1220 NORTH BOSWORTH AVENUE, CHICAGO, ILLINOIS

Enclosed find $.................................for.....................years subscription.

Name ....

Street ....

Town .... Zone.............. State ....

(Please do not send stamps)

Subscriptions are the backbone of a Bulletin. So help in "backing" the American Aid Societies Bulletin by mailing in your subscription TODAY.

Courtesy American Aid Society

Edward Mark O'Connor, AAS Bulletin

Truman specifically pointed to defects in Public Law 774. A particularly bad stipulation was the December 22, 1945, cut-off date, which meant that a large number of Jews who fled pogroms in Poland were excluded. Dinnerstein argues that

> The bill passed with the discriminatory provisions because antisemitism in the United States waxed strong, and its existence proved too formidable a barrier to overcome. Senator Revercomb and his allies knew exactly what they were doing when they inserted the December 22, 1945, cut-off date, and contemporaries criticized them for it.[71]

Truman also pointed to the feature for 'mortgaging' future immigration quotas, the forty percent preference for DP's from *de facto* annexed areas, the requirement for written assurances of both housing and jobs (which would not displace American citizens) before these people could come, and the necessity of 'affirmative action' by Congress in every instance where the Attorney General wanted to change the status of DP's already in the United States. Truman was clear when he said that he was only signing the bill, with its many 'defects', so that there would be no more delay in the resettlement activity. Later, when he called a special session of the Eighty-First Congress he included an attempt to introduce amendments to Public Law 774, but as we shall see, it wasn't going to be quite that easy for the President.

American Jewry was 'outraged' by the 1948 Displaced Persons Act. Dinnerstein remarks that

> There was a double irony in the 1948 DP Act. Not only did it discriminate against Jews but it undercut the advantages that had accrued to them under the provisions of the Truman Directive. Between May 1946, when the first boatload of refugees to be given preference under the President's order arrived, until June 29, 1948, Jews constituted about two-thirds of the 41,379 people admitted under the program. On July 1, 1948, when the new law went into effect, 23,000 European DP's (mostly Jews) who had received preliminary approval to enter the United States had their priorities wiped out because the act had specifically repealed the Truman Directive.[72]

For the *Donauschwaben* there was an even more difficult problem than the requirement for assurances or the cut-off dates. That portion of the Act which referred to them, Section 12, (which made provision for a 'German expellee' program lasting until July 1, 1952), did not come

---

[71] Dinnerstein, *America and the Survivors*, 175.

[72] Ibid., 181.

under the domain of the Displaced Persons Commission. Instead, they were assigned to the control of the State Department, far away from sympathetic Catholic friends.

CHAPTER FIVE

A HOUSE OUT OF THE RUINS

At the time of the signing of the Displaced Persons Act the *Schwobs* didn't know the extent of the problems they were still to face, especially within the State department bureaucracy. Accordingly, the first issue of the American Aid Societies *Bulletin* that came out of Chicago announced in big, bold letters:

LANDSLEUTE UMSIEDLUNG!

Resettlement. It was a word deeply rooted in their past. Even if only a small number could come to America, it meant that their people had come full circle. *Resettlement. Expulsion. Resettlement.* Furthermore, it meant nothing less than a chance to save their people within the context of what was, for them, a life and death situation.

In this first issue from the Chicago office the different roles of Nick Pesch and John Meiszner became clear. To Pesch fell the task of conscience for his people, and in his very first article entitled *'Aufwachen!'*, he revealed the hardened steel underneath his soft-spoken exterior. After briefly summarizing the three year long struggle to create the American Aid Societies and reiterating the terrible catastrophe that was befalling their people in Europe, Pesch launched into an attack on the *Schwobs* in the United States:

> It sometimes takes away our courage when we learn how indifferent the great majority of our Donauschwaben countrymen here are about the hopeless situation of our brothers and sisters in the old country, especially when we know that of the up to one hundred thousand Donauschwaben only a tiny fraction belong to our Relief Society. Our people in Europe, to whom we belong, are being totally robbed, driven out of house and home and homeland and completely wiped out. And here we are playing cards and standing at the

50

bar, or at our summer homes fishing. And this with peace in our souls, as if everything in the world were in perfect order.[73]

That the picture in Europe was indeed still terrible can be taken from the report of a field trip made in 1949 by Members of Congress to the American Zones of Occupation, which may help to explain the sting in Nick Pesch's words. An especially vivid paragraph of that report was but confirmation of what the Chicago *Schwobs* had been hearing since August 1944. The Congressmen observed:

> Hundreds of thousands of refugees have ingeniously contrived the semblance of a house out of the ruins. On a cold day, in every German city smoke can be seen emerging from stove pipes sticking up through the rubble, or at night, lights appear from chinks in houses which would be thought totally uninhabitable.[74]

Pesch knew exactly how to prod the proud *Schwobs*. He concluded his article with a threat that no self-respecting *Schwabenkind* would have been able to shrug off.

> If we leave our people in the lurch, and that's what it will look like, then it will be able to be said that there is something foul among the *Donauschwaben*.[75]

While Pesch was thus working the collective conscience of his people in America, John Meiszner busied himself with the details. His

---

[73] Nick Pesch, *Aufwachen!*, A.A.S. Bulletin, October 1948, Vol.1, No.2., 1-4. "Es wird einem manchmal gar arg[sic] Mute, wenn man erfaehrt, wie gleichgueltig die grosse Masse unserer donauschwaebischen Landsleute hierzulande der fast hoffnungslosen Lage unserer Brueder und Schwestern in der alten Heimat gegenuebersteht; namentlich wenn man weiss, das von den zu hunderttausenden zaehlenden Donauschwaben nur ein ganz geringer prozentsatz Mitglied einer Ortsgruppe unser Hilfsvereinigung ist. Ein Volksstamm, den man selber angehoert, wird in Europa total ausgeraubt, von seinem Hof und Haus und von seiner Heimat vertrieben, um gaenzlich vernichtet zu werden. Und hier ist man bei seinem Kartenspiel, steht an der Bar, oder man ist in seinem Sommerheim und angelt Fischen. Und das mit einer Seelenruhe, als waere die Welt in groesster Ordnung." Translated by author.

[74] *Expellees and Refugees of German Ethnic Origin,* Report of a Special Subcommittee of the Committee on the Judiciary, House of Representatives, 81st Congress, 2nd Session, Report #1841, March 24, 1950, 33.

[75] Nick Pesch, *Aufwachen!,* "Wenn wir sie im Stiche lassen, dann wird es wohl so aussehen. Dann, freilich, wird man uns sagen, es ist etwas faul- um die Donauschwaben." Translated by author.

was apparently a logistically oriented mind, providing a perfect counterweight to Pesch's spiritual and morally-focused thrust. In his section of the *Bulletin*, called 'From The Desk Of The Secretary', he gently chided the other Chapters for not responding to his requests for information. He explained the purpose of the *Bulletin*, publicity, and exhorted the Chapters to cooperate with the National Office. He discussed the cost of the publication and suggested that this cost could be defrayed if the 'members succeed to get more advertisement'.

The *Bulletin* also laid out for the *Donauschwaben* in America the exact legal meaning of the Displaced Persons Act with regard to the resettlement of their people. After mentioning logistical questions such as 'mortgaged' German and Austrian quotas, affidavits of support, and payment for travel, the discussion passed on to weightier matters. One key proviso regarding who would actually be allowed to immigrate to the United States under the DP Act was the *makellose Vergangenheit* (unblemished past) issue. The A.A.S. believed that

> Any person who has an unblemished personal history (who was not a Nazi) and is able to work, and has the necessary papers may get a visa.

The second critical proviso related to military service.

> Men who served in the military might also be resettled if they can produce two impartial references proving that they didn't go into the military of their own free will.[76]

In spite of all this, by November 1948, the Chicago *Schwobs* thought they had reason to celebrate. They felt sure they had played a part, however small, in winning a political victory by organizing, fund raising and creating alliances. They had a worthy cause which they were fighting for. They had a 'National Organization'. And they had a champion among the *Obrigkeit*. The headline of the November 1948, *Bulletin* was effusive. The Chicago Chapter was holding its 4th Annual Banquet. They were proud to announce:

---

[76] A.A.S. *Bulletin*, October 1948, Vol.1, No.2., " 6) Aussicht auf ein Visum hat jede person, die eine makellose Vergangenheit hat (nicht Nazi gewesen ist) arbeitsfaehig ist und die noetigen papiere (Affidavits) hat. 13) Maenner, die beim Militaer gedient haben, koennen auch umgesiedelt werden, wenn sie zwei desinteressierte Zeugen bringen, die es bestaetigen, dass der Betreffende nicht freiwillig zum Miltaer ging." Translated by author.

SENATOR WILLIAM LANGER TO BE IN CHICAGO

There would be a concert, speakers on immigration, dancing, and plenty of the simple, hearty food *Schwobs* love. They would also raffle off prizes, sending the profits to the relief workers in Europe. But most of all they would come to see Bill Langer in person.

Of this controversial man the journalist-novelist Allen Drury once wrote:

> He is an odd character, the maverick of the Senate, so proud of being turned out of the governorship of his state that he lists it in the *Congressional Directory* like an accolade. If his ideas have any value no one will ever know it, for he presents them at the top of his lungs like a roaring bull in the empty chamber, while such of his colleagues as remain watch him in half-amused, half-fearful silence, as though in the presence of an irresponsible force they can neither control nor understand. In some ways this Congress is a strange, strange thing, composed of the symbols of a people's erratic will.[77]

Photo courtesy American Aid Society

Senator William Langer with the *Schwobs*
at the Logan Square Masonic Temple December 12, 1948.

---

[77] Allen Drury, *A Senate Journal 1943-1945,*(New York: McGraw-Hill, 1963), 27.

This however, was not how the *Donauschwaben* saw Bill Langer. If Drury had gone to Chicago with the Senator, he would have seen another side of the Maverick. He would have seen Langer surrounded by people that thought him a 'great man'. He would have witnessed the 'roaring bull' holding hands with *Schwobs* in a decidedly paternalistic manner, an example of the classic American champion of the underdog.

Source: American Aid Society

The leadership of the A.A.S., Logan Square Masonic Temple, December 12, 1948. Seated: John Meiszner, Sam Baumann, Nick Pesch. The refrigerator behind Senator Langer was being raffled off.

This was really the first major American politician either to fight for them or to descend from Capitol Hill to their world, and they made the most of the opportunity. They honored Langer as best they could in the humble surroundings of the Logan Square Masonic Temple. From the photographs we are privy to the other Langer, the one Drury clearly did not understand when he wrote in 1945:

> There is a disturbing sense about him, somewhere underneath the very smooth heartiness and the firm, lingering handshake, that here is a man of great violence and great anger. I have seen how it comes out on the floor, it dissipates itself into howling nothingness, but it is only luck that it does so. If

it did not, here might be a man as dangerous in his way as Huey Long in his, one of those wild, harsh men out of the wild harsh places of America, uncontrollable and elemental. He lacks the essential quality of appeal to the masses, but aside from that he was built for power- too much power. It is the nation's good fortune that he will never achieve it.[78]

Source: American Aid Society

The Chicago *Schwobs* at the Logan Square Masonic Temple,
December 12, 1948

A more fitting description of why Langer sided with the *Donauschwaben* could probably not have been written. Drury, in his role as a journalist, simply never bothered to investigate further the causes of Langer's fury. He settled for the outward appearances of William Langer. And yet, in his complaint lies precisely that which Langer and the *Schwobs* shared, especially the 'great anger' which 'dissipates itself into howling nothingness'.

On October 24, 1948, the *New York Times Magazine* ran an article about *'The Lost and Forgotten Children of Europe'*. The cover photograph showed two hungry little boys with eyes that could break

---

[78] Ibid, 33.

hearts. Inside, the article showed children without shoes in Budapest, and war-mutilated children in a Rome schoolroom. One boy, eleven years old, was blind and missing both arms, reading Braille with his tongue. They were wrenching images.

Source: *The New York Times Magazine*, Oct 24, 1948

Haunting image of a hungry child

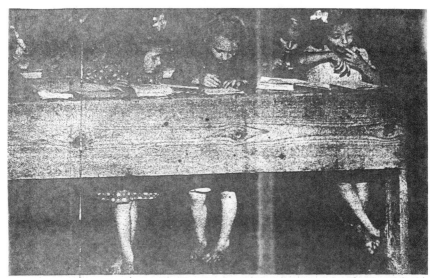

Symbolizing the crucial lack of just one necessity—shoes—in France, Italy, Hungary, Czechoslovakia, Austria, is this picture taken in a crude, one-room schoolhouse near Budapest. The teacher of this second-grade class explained that "many of these children won't be able to come to school this winter because they can't walk barefoot on icy roads."

Source: *The New York Times Magazine*, October 24, 1948

The barefoot children of Budapest. .

The Lost and Forgotten Children of Europe

Source: *The New York Times Magazine*, October 24, 1948

War-mutilated children.

What was worse was that by this time even the resettlement victory was proving to be hollow, as was seen when the first DP transport ship came to the United States.

> The *General Black* arrived in New York Harbor on October 30, 1948. As the transport went up New York Harbor the newcomers stood on deck and sought out the Statue of Liberty and the tall buildings of New York City.
> The 'somewhat shopworn-looking ship with a rusty grey hull and flecks of dirt on its white superstructure' received a harbor welcome which one observer declared was usually 'reserved before the war for superliners and after the war for returning American soldiers.' An Army tug sailed around the ship with a banner reading 'Welcome to America'.[79]

Of these 813 displaced persons who had sailed from Bremerhaven there were Poles, Czechs, Ukrainians, Latvians and even six Hungarians.

---

[79] Ibid, 64.

There were no German expellees. For Nick Pesch and the others it had now been over four years since the nightmare of the *Donauschwaben* had begun.

DP'S RISE IN DARK FOR SIGHT OF CITY

Last Day on Transport Begins at 4 A. M.—Greetings Leave Them In Happy Daze

By HAROLD FABER

The 813 displaced persons coming to waiting jobs, homes and eventual citizenship in the United States, were happy but inarticulate when the General Black docked here yesterday. Many of them could not speak English, but those who did repeated phrases such as "It's wonderful," "It's beautiful" and simply, "I'm glad to be here."

The arrival of the ship in New York ended a nine-day trip from Bremerhaven, Germany, and a search for a new home that began for some as long as nine years ago when Germany invaded Poland to start World War II.

The DP's first day in the United States began at 4 A. M. when, unable to sleep, they arose, washed, cleaned their cabins and went topside to watch for America. Shortly after 1 P. M. some had sighted fishing boats and glimpses of the Long Island shore.

As the transport passed the Ambrose Lightship and up New York harbor, the newcomers, like all who arrived before them, searched out the Statue of Liberty, and began exclaiming at the tall buildings.

Dressed in the best of their small supply of clothing, they lined the rails and applauded loudly as Ugo Carusi, head of the United States Displaced Persons Commission, and

AS FIRST BOATLOAD OF DISPLACED PERSONS REACHED AMERICA

Crowding along the rail of the transport General Black to get a view of the skyline

Source: *The New York Times*, October 31, 1948

The arrival of the U.S.S. General Black.

CHAPTER SIX

THE CLOGGED PIPELINE

Many complex reasons explain why there were no German expellees on the *U.S.S. General Black.* To begin with, the entire undertaking was new in U.S. immigration history. The process of setting up the organizational superstructure, administering it in Europe and in the U.S., defining legal terms set forth in the DP Act, designing forms, creating procedures and promulgating regulations, hiring staff, appropriating funds and coordinating with the various governmental bodies involved, European and American, required an entire book to document. In fact, the Displaced Persons Commission had a Chief Historian on staff to write the 376 page *Memo to America: The DP Story. The Final Report of The United States Displaced Persons Commission*, as required by the Act itself. This governmental book, while essentially a defense, nevertheless documents this remarkable episode in American immigration history. It also tells us about the unique struggle of the German expellees within that period.

In spite of the *Berliner Luft Brücke* and the mitigating impact of Truman's presidency on the American *Zeitgeist* with regard to DP's, the atmosphere was still supercharged as far as Germans were concerned. It would be some time before the German expellees could also be categorized as part of 'the deserving, suffering victims of totalitarian aggression, the front line troops of democracy'.[80] For now they were much more under the shadow of Section 13 of the Displaced Persons Act which

> ...provided that no person should receive a visa who had been a member of or participated in any movement hostile to the United States or its form of government...[81]

---

[80] *Second Semiannual Report to the President and the Congress,* The Displaced Persons Commission, August 1, 1949, 1.

[81] Memo to America: The DP Story, 100.

The DP Commission created a secret master list which included Communist, Nazi and Fascist organizations and which served as the guide used by the Immigration and Naturalization Service, the State Department, the Counter Intelligence Corps and the Criminal Investigations Division of the U.S. Army. This was the only, and therefore, the definitive list compiled by the U.S. Government. It was the first hurdle any applicant had to leap. For the German expellees it was a difficult barrier. For Nick Pesch and the *Donauschwaben* the question was: How could the *Volksdeutsche* have avoided joining some form of organization which was now classified as 'hostile' when Hitler took power in these countries? For the *Schwobs* it seemed unjust to exclude *Ungarndeutsche* who had been forced to join in either military or pseudo-cultural organizations.

A typical example of the work Nick Pesch and John Meiszner were doing throughout this rescue is the case of the Stumpf family. Mrs. Maria Stumpf was an American-born woman who had become a refugee from Yugoslavia along with her husband Thomas and their daughter Magdalena. Being American-born, she had been allowed to come to the U.S. after the war. She naturally wanted her husband and daughter back. On March 29, 1949, she received notification that her petition for issuance of an immigration visa had been approved and forwarded to the State Department. On May 23, 1949, John Meiszner wrote to the American Consul in Stuttgart and tried to explain why Thomas Stumpf could not produce birth and marriage certificates. Their town had been destroyed and burned and the records were ashes.

On June 1, 1949, Meiszner received letters from the Immigration and Naturalization Service, and the National Catholic Welfare Conference's Bureau of Immigration. The letter from INS informed him that his inquiry regarding Stumpf was being forwarded to the Visa Division of the State Department, whose jurisdiction this case fell under. The letter from NCWC came from the Port Director, New York, T.F. Mulholland, who informed him that the Stumpfs would not qualify for free transportation from the IRO. He suggested that Maria Stumpf make her own transportation arrangements.

On June 8, 1949, Pan American World Airways wrote Mrs. Stumpf and asked her if she was willing to pay for her husband and daughter to ride one of the Flying Clippers. On June 9, 1949, the Chief of the Visa

File No.: 211-Stumpf, Thomas
MIT/ej

'HE FOREIGN SERVICE
OF THE
UNITED STATES OF AMERICA

ADDRESS OFFICIAL COMMUNICATIONS TO

AMERICAN CONSULATE,

Stuttgart, Germany, June 20, 1949.

Mr. John C. Meiszner, Secretary,
American Aid Societies for the Needy and
Displaced Persons of Central and South-
Eastern Europe.
5622-24 Irving Park Road,
Chicago 34, Illinois.

Sir:

Receipt is acknowledged of your letter of May 23,
1949 which has reference to the desire of Mr. Thomas
Stumpf and his daughter, Magdalena, to immigrate to
the United States.

Information on file at this office indicates that,
because of service as a non-commissioned officer in
the Waffen SS, Mr. Stumpf is inadmissible to the United
States under the provisions of Section 53.53 k, Chapter (Title)
22, Code of Federal Regulations, relating to aliens
whose entry is deemed to be prejudicial to the interests
of the United States. It appears that Miss Magdalena
Stumpf is admissible to the United States.

The Consulate is notifying Mr. Stumpf today of
its findings, and has asked him to indicate whether
he wishes to withdraw his application for visa or if
he desires to file formal application therefor, in
which latter event the Consulate will be constrained
to withhold the issuance of a visa to him.

Very truly yours,

For the Consul General:

.. B. Lundgren
American Vice Consul

Source: American Aid Society Records: used with permission

Letter from the American Vice Consul to John Meiszner June 20, 1949

Division of the State Department wrote Meiszner and informed him that
the Consular Officer at Stuttgart had been authorized on April 1, 1949,
to grant non-quota visas to Thomas and Magdalena. On June 17, 1949,
Maria Stumpf went to the Weiss Travel Bureau on West North Avenue
and paid for two plane tickets from Stuttgart to Milwaukee. The price
was $940.84.

So far everything was going well. On June 20, 1949, all that changed. The American Vice Consul in Stuttgart wrote John Meiszner and informed him that:

> Information on file at this office indicates that, because of service as a non-commissioned officer in the Waffen S.S., Mr. Stumpf is inadmissible to the United States under the provisions of Section 53.53 k, Chapter 22, Code of Federal Regulations, relating to aliens whose entry is deemed to be prejudicial to the interests of the United States. It appears that Miss Magdalena Stumpf is admissible to the United States.[82]

In spite of this terrible news, Meiszner and Maria Stumpf still pressed forward. At least they would be able to bring the daughter out. Meiszner sent a Western Union Night Letter on August 16, 1949, wondering why Magdalena hadn't received her visa yet.

> Her mother Maria Stumpf greatly concerned, it being beyond her and our understanding, that by and beyond September 3, 1949, when Magdalena reaches age 21, she will no longer be admitted as a non-quota immigrant.[83]

On August 26, 1949, the Chief of the Visa Division informed Meiszner that Magdalena was invited to call at the consulate for the purpose of filing her 'formal application for a visa'. A note scribbled on this letter in red pencil marked the conclusion of this particular half-won bureaucratic battle. It said simply:

Miss Stumpf arrived 8/28/49.

At this juncture Nick Pesch got into the situation. He targeted a lawmaker with a large German constituency when he wrote to Congressman Earl T. Wagner of Cincinnati, Ohio on September 23, 1949:

> At the time of the war trials in Nurnberg, denazification cases en masse, against 'Volksdeutsche' (D.P.'s of Ethnic German Origin) were dismissed, when lawyers for the defense proved, that these men were forced into S.S.

---

[82] Letter to John C. Meiszner, A.A.S. Records, Danube Swabian Cultural Center, Lake Villa, Illinois.

[83] Letter to John C. Meiszner, A.A.S. Records, Danube Swabian Cultural Center, Lake Villa, Illinois.

ADDRESS OFFICIAL COMMUNICATIONS TO
THE SECRETARY OF STATE
WASHINGTON 25, D. C.

DEPARTMENT OF STATE
WASHINGTON

Miss Stumpf
arrived 8/28/49

In reply refer to
VD 811.111 Stumpf, Magdelena

~~August 26 1949~~

American Aid Society,

    1220 North Bosworth Avenue,

        Chicago, Illinois.

Sirs:

    The Department is in receipt of a telegram from
the American Consulate at Stuttgart, Germany, dated
August 22, 1949, concerning the immigration visa case
of Miss Magdalena Stumpf.

    The consular officer requests that you be informed
that Miss Stumpf was invited to call at the Consulate
on August 25, 1949 for the purpose of filing her formal
application for a visa.

        Very truly yours,

                    H. J. L'Heureux
              Chief, Visa Division

Courtesy: American Aid Society

Letter from H.J. L'Heureux to John Meiszner, August 26, 1949

service and therefore could not be considered Nazis. We think that this should
clarify them Non-Nazis in this country also.

...Under the present immigration laws and regulations, all former S.S.
members are barred from entree [sic] into this country, regardless of the

circumstances connected. Please look into this matter in order to enable these
men to be admitted to this country, when they make the request.[84]

It would take one full year for the nature of legal definitions and the
process of research and refinement to rectify this situation. The DP
Commission finally fought out into open ground over the issue of the
Baltic Waffen SS. The Chief Historian admitted:

> One of the organizations which was the subject of considerable controversy
> with respect to the effect of membership in it was the Baltic *Waffen SS*,
> otherwise known as the Baltic Legion. Membership in the Baltic Legion was
> for several years considered by both the Commission and the Visa Division to
> be a bar *per se* under the security provisions of section 13 of the Act. After
> extensive research and review, and on the basis of a change of view by the
> Visa Division, and strong evidence showing that membership in the
> organization was due to conscription and force by the Hitler regime, the
> Commission revised its policy on September 1, 1950, by holding the Baltic
> Legion not to be a movement hostile to the United States under section 13 of
> the Act. This view was not a unanimous decision within the Commission; an
> extensively documented statement of the minority views was filed by
> Commissioner Rosenfield.[85]

How large a part Nick Pesch and John Meiszner played in this
process of revision, if any, is not known, but it is certain that as two of
the voices speaking for the German expellees, they had some impact.
The NCWC, War Relief Services Director, Monsignor Edward
Swanstrom, kept Pesch informed of upcoming bills and urged him to
keep the legislative pots boiling. Meiszner and Pesch spent a lot of
money and many hours standing at the Western Union counter,
methodically sending telegrams to each and every Congressman and
Senator on Capitol Hill in the name of the '12 chapters in major
American cities'.

The DPC chose to call the resettlement process the 'Pipeline'. For
the *Schwobs* the Pipeline was clogged with red tape, especially because,
according to the Chief Historian's own words:

---

[84] Pesch Letter to Earl T. Wagner, September 23, 1949, Pesch Letters, A.A.S. Records,
Danube Swabian Cultural Center, Lake Villa, Illinois.
[85] Memo to America: The DP Story, 102.

The Commission established the most rigorous system of security and intelligence investigations in the history of American immigration.[86]

The list of security agencies the applicants had to go through is quite remarkable. Again, the Commission's own book says it best when it claims that:

...to ensure against undesirable and subversive aliens, every applicant under the Act was checked by:

(a) The Federal Bureau of Investigation.
(b) The Counter-Intelligence Corps of the United States Army, which included 21 separate investigative steps before submitting its report to the Commission.
(c) The Central Intelligence Agency
(d) The Provost-Marshal General of the United States Army in Germany.
(e) The fingerprint record center in Heidelberg, Germany.
(f) The Berlin Document Center.
(g) A special investigation in connection with displaced persons whose country of origin had been overrun by Communists.
(h) A special additional check by the Immigration and Naturalization Service of the Department of Justice through stationing of its immigration inspectors overseas in the DP Resettlement Centers as well as at ports of entry.
(i) A check by consular officers especially assigned for this program.
(j) In addition, by special liaison investigations with British Intelligence in the British Zone of Germany, France's Surete General in the French Zone of Germany, and Italy's Questura.[87]

Although Dinnerstein argues that the security personnel doing this work were often poorly trained and that slipshod work let Nazi collaborators get through, it is doubtful that many German expellees managed to get past all of these checks, especially since they had to identify themselves as ethnic Germans. This kind of scrutiny, coupled with the inter-agency immigration authority over the fate of applicants led to some ironic situations. Under the Displaced Persons Act one of the legal criteria hinged upon the phrase of 'good character'. Under Immigration law the phrase 'moral turpitude' was operative. When applied to the scene in postwar Europe it worked out strangely. An actual case from the DPC Report is illustrative.

---

[86] Ibid, 102.
[87] Ibid, 100.

An applicant for admission to the United States had stolen a loaf of bread to feed his hungry family, during the very difficult and trying circumstances of the immediate postwar period. For this he had been tried and convicted. The Commission found such a person, under those circumstances and in the light of his conduct subsequent to that incident, to be of 'good character' and passed the case on to the consuls. This it did because, on principle, it could administer only the Displaced Persons Act and not the immigration law, which was for the consuls and the immigrant inspectors to interpret and administer. In this case, the applicant had to be denied a visa by the consul because of a crime involving moral turpitude.[88]

We can imagine this man walking out of the Consulate, barred forever from immigrating to the United States, shaking his head at the situation which meant that one American immigration agency had meticulously investigated him and weighed the 'moral turpitude' involved in his crime, judging him to be of 'good character', while the other immigration agency could not take any of that extensive inquiry into consideration. We can only wonder if he asked anyone at the Consulate which act involved greater moral turpitude, stealing a loaf of bread or letting his family starve.

After an applicant had run this unprecedented gauntlet, the person still had to clear the Public Health Service doctors. A person could go through the entire process and be rejected for ill health at this stage. This dilemma left people with the choice to leave someone behind so that the whole family wouldn't suffer, or stay together. It was a human drama replayed countless times as people put themselves into the DPC Pipeline, hoping to be shoved out on the other end into a different world. For the German expellees it was to prove a long, narrow pipe, one which

...stretched anywhere from 3 to more than 12 months, sometimes because of the nature of the case itself, always because of the complexity of the legal requirements and the thoroughness of the security investigation.[89]

The DPC was continuously complaining to the President and the Congress about "...the unworkability of the entire pattern of restrictions, limitations, preferences, and priorities established by the law."[90]

---

[88] Ibid, 173.
[89] Ibid, 76.
[90] 2nd Semiannual Report, DPC, Aug.1949, 2.

One of those legal requirements was what had been called the *Baltic Preference*, meaning that 40% of the visas had to go to displaced persons from *de facto* annexed areas. Meaning strictly the countries of Estonia, Latvia and Lithuania, as well as the Free City of Danzig, this meant that 40% of the visas would go to 19% of the displaced population. The DPC decided that this was unacceptable and used two methods to circumvent this unreasonable provision. First, it adopted a policy of 'first come, first served' with regard to assurances

> ...on the theory that periodic compliance with these ratios was unnecessary just so long as there was compliance with these ratios by the end of the program.[91]

Essentially the DPC stalled the Baltic preference while it went back to Congress for revision of the DP Act. It was a good example of bureaucratic battle tactics, but the second circumvention was even better.

Using the term *de facto annexed areas*, the DPC went to the State Department and asked for an 'official' definition of annexed areas. This maneuver greatly expanded the territories available.

> The de facto annexed countries and territories contained in the Department of State's definition are located in eastern Europe and include those whose transfer to other powers have not been recognized by the United States Government. In the main, the countries and territories comprised within the definition are those which are now under the rule of a power other than the one which exercised sovereignty in 1937...[92]

This move allowed the DPC to include all of the countries swallowed up by the U.S.S.R. when issuing the allocated 'annexed' visas. From the very outset then, it becomes clear that the three men in charge of the Displaced Persons Commission were following the Truman line. Both the President and the DPC wanted to bring people out of the devastating situation in Europe, whatever the reasons, and both of them were confronting the problem with the same vigor. As Leonard Dinnerstein observed:

> Jews who anticipated few positive effects from the 1948 Displaced Persons Act would be quite surprised to see how the new law was administered. They considered the legislation restrictive and could have no way of knowing in June

---

[91] Ibid, 12.
[92] Ibid, 12.

that the commissioners later appointed by the President in August would be imaginative in their interpretations of the bill's provisions. In fact, the DPC was so creative in its operations that many legislators would later wonder how the bill that they had voted for contained so many loopholes.[93]

Commissioner Edward O'Connor, who was specifically charged with the resettlement section of the DPC, operating within his Catholic framework, nevertheless echoed Truman's concerns about Communism. An official DPC press release of June 17, 1951 reveals O'Connor's feelings:

> The masters in the Kremlin and their elite functionaries are guilty of a long list of crimes against humanity and the day is inevitable when they must be tried before a world tribunal of justice, Edward M. O'Connor, Washington, D.C., Commissioner of Displaced Persons, said in Carnegie Hall...[94]

Even though the President of the United States was concerned about the instability of a Europe jammed full homeless, hungry and hopeless millions and many with him were doing all they could to alleviate the situation, from the Swabian viewpoint, even this did not seem to be helping them. In the *2nd Semiannual Report* the statistics told a bitter story. Visas issued from Austria, Germany, Hungary, Rumania and Yugoslavia amounted to 316. This meant 16 people from Hungary, 29 from Rumania, 2 from Yugoslavia, 9 from Austria and 260 from annexed German territories. By contrast, Poland sent 11,516, Lithuania 8,609, Latvia 4,998, Estonia 2,438, and Czechoslovakia 838. The Great Chicago Refugee Rescue still hadn't happened.

---

[93] Dinnerstein, *America and the Survivors*, 182.
[94] DPC Press Release, June 17,1951, DPC Document, A.A.S. Records, Danube Swabian Cultural Center, Lake Villa, Illinois.

CHAPTER SEVEN

DP STANDS FOR DELAYED PILGRIM[95]

Miss Magdalena Stumpf had been fortunate. By August 1949, very few *Schwobs* had been taken out of Europe. The reasons for this delay could be found within the very agency empowered to administer the German expellee program. From the date of enactment of the DP Act, June 25, 1948, until February 1949, the State Department could not come up with an administrative definition of who qualified to be called of *German ethnic origin*. The Chief of the Visa Division of the State Department, Mr. H.J.L'Heureux then informally requested the Committees of the Judiciary of the Senate and the House to examine his definition. This tactic, while partially deflecting criticism by bringing the Congress into the delay, actually speeded things up. In less than a month both Chambers acted. By March 1949, when the definition finally appeared, it seemed incredibly simple to have taken so long to formulate.

In order to qualify an expellee merely had to show:
1. That he was born in Poland, Czechoslovakia, Hungary, Rumania, or Yugoslavia...
2. That he resided in any part of Germany or Austria on June 25, 1948...
3. That he does not come under the jurisdiction of the International Refugee Organization...
4. (a) That he is a German expellee, or the accompanying wife or minor child of a German expellee, pursuant to the Potsdam Agreement of August 1, 1945; or (b) that he is a refugee, or the accompanying wife or minor child of a refugee from Poland, Czechoslovakia, Hungary, Rumania, or Yugoslavia...
5. That he is characteristically Germanic...[96]

---

[95] Supposedly coined by William Bernard of the CCDP for its 'favorable connotation' as opposed to 'Displaced Person', Dinnerstein, *America and the Survivors*, 160.

[96] *Administrative Definition Of The Term "German Ethnic Origin" As Used In Section 12 Of The Displaced Persons Act Of June 25, 1948.* State Department Document, American Aid Society Records, Lake Villa, Illinois.

L'Heureux's manoeuvre worked to his advantage later when he submitted a memorandum of defense to the Special Subcommittee of the Committee on the Judiciary, House of Representatives, on January 27, 1950, which was by now investigating immigration and nationality problems pursuant to House Resolution 238. In their concluding remarks the Congressmen used this memorandum as they sought answers for the incredible delay in admitting German expellees. Their report quoted L'Heureux as saying:

> ...there was considerable difficulty with the question of administrative possibility of a definition on the basis of which applicants could be classified as persons of German ethnic origin. Through the greatly appreciated cooperation of members of the subcommittees of both Chambers of Congress, that problem was in March 1949, resolved by a definition approved informally by both subcommittees. On the basis of this definition, we were able to give the consuls instructions on how to classify applicants as persons of German ethnic origin.[97]

This situation meant that nine irretrievable months had already been used up on nothing more substantial than red tape. Of the 13,685 German expellees who were authorized to come that first year, 165 people had actually made it.[98]

In April 1949, the Displaced Persons Commission held a national conference at the Stevens Hotel in Chicago:

> For the first time the public agencies, represented by the then 23 state commissions and committees, were able to meet with the 13 American voluntary agencies accredited by the Commission. Also in attendance were representatives of seven interested departments and agencies of the Federal Government.[99]

While the American Aid Societies did not qualify as one of the thirteen 'accredited' voluntary agencies, which included powerful groups like the Hebrew Sheltering and Immigrant Aid Society, the *Schwobs* did have an inside, Catholic connection through the National Catholic Welfare

---

[97] L'Heureux memorandum in *Expellees and Refugees of German Ethnic Origin*, Report of a Special Subcommittee of the Committee on the Judiciary, House of Representatives, Report No.1841, 81st Congress, 2nd Session, 85.

[98] Memo to America: The DP Story, 78.

[99] Displaced Persons Commission, 2nd Report, 20. See also: House Document No.220, 81st Congress, 1st Session.

Conference, which was one of the thirteen. Swanstrom frequently telegrammed Pesch and Meiszner and informed them of upcoming conferences. By this time the American Aid Societies had been present at National Catholic Resettlement Conferences held in New York and Boston.

The two *Schwobs* from Chicago were developing useful relationships with Monsignor Edward E.Swanstrom and Edward O'Connor, thus gaining entrance into the two offices most able to effect a change in this unacceptable situation. Swanstrom, in his role as the Executive Director of War Relief Services of the NCWC was at the head of a powerful lobby, which had been granted accredited agency status by the DPC, but he still needed the sponsors and the legislative pressure which groups like the A.A.S. could provide.

In his role as the Commissioner in charge of Resettlement, Edward O'Connor had the exact same needs as he was poised to confront the Congress in the upcoming battle to amend the DP Act of 1948. This symbiotic relationship would prove to be critical for the Chicago *Schwobs*.

The National Resettlement Conference For Displaced Persons held at the Hotel Stevens in Chicago on April 5, 6, and 7, 1949, was a watershed event for Pesch and Meiszner. This conference hosted all three DP Commissioners, Ugo Carusi, Edward O'Connor and Harry Rosenfield. Representatives of various state Displaced Persons Commissions were speakers, as were bureaucrats concerned with every aspect of the DP issue. The assistant to the Director of the U.S. Department of Agriculture spoke, as did the Assistant Director of the U.S. Employment Service, the Commissioner of the Immigration and Naturalization Service, the Director of the Bureau of Employment Security of the Social Security Administration, the Director of the Bureau of Labor Standards of the U.S. Department of Labor, the Commissioner of the U.S. Office of Education, the Operations Officer of the International Refugee Organization, the Chairman of the American Council of Voluntary Agencies for Foreign Service, and the European Coordinator for the DPC.

Nick Pesch, John Meiszner and other prominent Schwobs with Displaced Persons Commissioners Edward M. O'Connor and John W. Gibson. Note the hand sign Nick Pesch is giving the camera.

1. Joseph Sternbauer 2. Sam Baumann 3. Nick Pesch 4. Edward M. O'Connor 5. Math Gatsch 6. Matt Bastion 7. Joe Kunst 8. Alphonse Scheeman 9. Albert Gumbert 10. John W. Gibson 11. Peter Paul Reiner 12. Frank Wert 13. Timothy Sheehan 14. John Meiszner 15. John Schirmang 16. Josef Esterle 17. Martin Gerhardt

Source: A.A.S. Records

Monsignor Edward Swanstrom, Executive Director, War Relief Services, National Catholic Welfare Conference, at 6th Annual Banquet of the American Aid Societies, December 10, 1950.

Twenty-three states had full-fledged Displaced Persons Commissions by now, and 24 states had some kind of representation at this conference. There were seven working committees appointed on the first day to work out problem areas like rural resettlement, the relationship of the voluntary agencies to the State DP Commissions, the placement of DP's with professional skills, assurances and public charge provisions. There was even a Committee on Minimum Planning Within State for Reception, Good Resettlement, Education, and Americanization.

So important was this conference that Congressman Emanuel Celler, Chairman of the House of Representatives Committee on the Judiciary wrote DPC Commissioner Ugo Carusi on May 25, 1949, to request a copy of the proceedings so that he could print them up. He wanted them spread around the Congress prior to the debates over H.R. 4567,(the proposed amendments to the Displaced Persons Act of 1948).

Edward M. O'Connor delivered the opening address. He said:

The Chicago *Schwobs* with Commissioner John W. Gibson,
who took over when Ugo Carusi resigned.

In our day we find the spotlight of world opinion turned on our way of life. One arc of this spotlight seeks honestly to learn more about our system of government by the people wherein unparalleled freedom and personal opportunity prevail. Another arc is searching only for the opportunity to discredit the high principles upon which our way of life is built so as to turn from us the masses of people the world over who look to our leadership and assistance in restoring peace with freedom and opportunity for all. The resettlement of displaced persons in the United States is one means of demonstrating to the world that we as a Nation are not cold to the problems of the little man or any group of people who hold human freedoms more precious than anything else in life.[100]

The Commissioner also recognized that voluntary agencies had long before begun the work of feeding, clothing and caring for the medical needs of the displaced persons. O'Connor said:

Being close to the displaced persons themselves they came to know their problems intimately and, therefore, were among the first to recognize that there

---

[100]   Edward M. O'Connor, House Document No.220, 81st Congress, 1st Session, *Proceedings of the National Resettlement Conference for Displaced Persons*, 1.

would be a "hard core' who could not be repatriated and for whom new homelands would have to be found. This accounts in large measure for the fact that today they are admirably organized and well prepared to participate in the resettlement program...[101]

It is reasonable to assume that Nick Pesch and John Meiszner could applaud these remarks, especially when the Commissioner announced as the very first objective of the conference to be

To simplify present procedures in initiating assurances: All of us recognize that there is altogether too much paper work involved in our present practice which is not only time consuming but in many cases an additional expense.[102]

This was indeed an important change, something they could relate to in a conference overshadowed by another aspect of the Displaced Persons Act, that of bringing in the thousands of workers who had been requested by American employers. It was the delay in this massive manpower operation that most concerned the Commissioners.

Of the 205,000 DPs called for in the DP Act, by March, 1949, the DPC had over 115,000 assurances on file, and they were pouring in at the rate of approximately 5,000 a week. The most problematic of these assurances were the ones for unnamed DP's, in other words, DP's who were designated for some specific job, as opposed to the type of assurances the *Schwobs* and other voluntary agencies generally provided, which were for specifically named persons. Many of the American people viewed the DP Act as a way of getting grateful laborers for their farms, factories, homes and businesses. A primary thrust of the legislation was Americentric in that it was employment related, and the delays caused immense disillusionment among U.S. employers who were willing to sponsor a DP, provided he could do the work, could arrive on the job quickly, and have a good attitude when he got there.

The long delays meant that a prospective sponsor, like a dairy farmer seeking a farmhand, a doctor seeking a house servant, or a factory owner seeking a machinist, had to keep the job open and the housing unoccupied for long months while they waited for some DP they didn't know to arrive and assume his duties. It was this situation which

---

[101] Ibid, 4.
[102] Ibid, 5.

created an uproar among the sponsors. What made things even worse were those times when the DP finally got there, took one look around at the dismal quarters the farmer had set up for him and headed out for the city; or when the doctor's maid left for a better doctor's mansion; or when the machinist became really Americanized and found out that the Land of Opportunity also meant that another machine-shop was willing to pay him twice what he was making at his sponsor's facility.

All of this worked in the *Schwobs* favor. These pressures were molding the DPC into a streamlined organization, one with the factual weapons to demand changes. Harry N. Rosenfield, the Commissioner charged with the legal duties within the DPC got specific about these changes when he spoke at the conference. He stated:

> ...it is for these and other reasons that the Displaced Persons Commission has recommended an amendment to the present law which would delete these rigid employment and housing assurances, and substitute instead a requirement for assurances of reasonable and suitable resettlement opportunities...[103]

The *Schwobs* and others, like the Hebrew Sheltering and Immigrant Aid Society and the National Catholic Welfare Conference were recognized as working out of different motivational paradigms than employers, and were accordingly given what was called the blanket assurance. This was a grant of the DPC whereby

> ...because of the nature, integrity, and purpose of certain voluntary agencies they have been authorized by the Commission to submit "blanket" assurances, so to speak, which merely indicate the general nature of the employment, and the community in which the housing is to be provided. They need not specify the particular job, nor the particular employer, nor the specific housing to be provided.[104]

Essentially the DPC put the voluntary agencies on the honor system because they saw that DP's brought in by them would be lovingly cared for. Although the American Aid Societies could not qualify as one of these accredited agencies, they were to be permitted to submit blanket assurances under the auspices of their big Catholic friend, the NCWC.

---

[103] Harry N. Rosenfield, speech at National Resettlement Conference, April 5, 1949, in House Document No.220, 81st Congress, 1st Session, 8.
[104] Ibid, 9.

There were a few speakers at this conference whose speeches Pesch and Meiszner must have really applauded. One example are the remarks of Alexander Squadrilli, the Acting European Coordinator for the DPC who asserted:

> As I describe to you our system of operation, I hope you will not be offended by my use of terms such as "pipe line" and "production." I can assure you that few of us, if any, ever forget that we are treating with human beings. I can assure you also, that we are possessed with a driving sense of urgency, that we feel ourselves in a race against time, not only because of the limitation of the Displaced Persons Act, but because through long association we are only too sadly aware of the material and moral plight of the displaced persons and of the strain under which they labor in the current state of political uncertainty... If you could but feel the pressure that prevails at Bremen among the displaced persons eager to depart...[105]

The speaker who spoke loudest for Pesch, Meiszner and the *Schwobs* was Earl J. McGrath, the U.S. Commissioner of Education:

> One day in September 1946 I stood near the Austrian border and watched groups of displaced persons move westward into the American zone. They were a depressing sight. Their bodies had been beaten by cruel oppressors and emaciated from lack of food, their minds confused by the impact of conflicting doctrines, and their spirits depressed by the loss of kith and kin, and home and country. No one could have observed this steadily flowing stream of humanity without wishing that something could be done to help these fellow human beings whose plight was usually no fault of their own.[106]

Pesch and Meiszner were two of those 'observing this steadily flowing stream of humanity' and, as this conference closed, could certainly have been 'wishing that something could be done to help these fellow human beings.' It had been a long time since Kaspar Muth's letter had come to Chicago.

---

[105] Ibid, 14-17.
[106] Ibid, 44.

CHAPTER EIGHT

POWER OVER THE MATERIAL WORLD

The 81st Congress was busy fighting over the DP Act well before the National Resettlement Conference in Chicago. Thirty-two bills were introduced to amend the Displaced Persons Act, notably two by Bill Langer. On June 3, 1949 Congressman Emanuel Celler's bill, H.R. 4567, passed the House of Representatives. It was the best that the *Schwobs* of America could hope for under the circumstances.

H.R. 4567 increased the DP numbers from 205,000 to 339,000, which included nearly 18,000 Polish Army veterans who were living in England. This bill moved the cut-off date even further ahead than the DPC was officially requesting, from December 22, 1945 to January 1, 1949. The Baltic preference was to be scrapped, along with the 30% preference for farmers. Celler suggested a loan program to help sponsors with transport costs. But above all, H.R. 4567 increased the numbers of German expellees to 54,744, admittedly a minuscule amount compared with the 12,000,000 in Europe, but twice what the *Schwobs* then had. Celler's argument for his bill was forceful. Nick Pesch and John Meiszner put the A.A.S. squarely behind the NCWC in vigorously supporting this bill.

> Representative Celler emphasized the discriminatory character of the 1948 Act, and stated that under the President's directive, 42,000 persons had been admitted from December 22, 1945, to July 1, 1948, while only 2,499 persons had been admitted under the Displaced Persons Act.[107]

Cellar's efforts in the House were counterbalanced by opposing forces in the Senate. This time the isolationists, restrictionists and nativists found a champion of their own in the Democratic Senator from Nevada, Pat McCarran. Dinnerstein writes:

---

[107] Memo to America: The DP Story, 29.

The Democratic victory the previous November had put Cellar of Brooklyn into the House Judiciary chairmanship, just as it had elevated McCarran to the same position in the Senate. The New Yorker's position diametrically differed from the Nevadan's on DP legislation. Just as McCarran had chosen an immigration subcommittee whose majority wanted to block further immigration, Cellar's choices for the House Subcommittee on Immigration reflected his desire to liberalize the law.[108]

The DPC naturally supported Celler, although they wanted a few additions of their own. They sought the changes Commissioner Rosenfield had mentioned regarding assurances, the discontinuation of quota mortgaging, increasing the numbers to 400,000 for a 4 year period instead of two, and most important of all for the *Schwobs*, that "a technical transfer be made of the German expellee program."[109]

Pesch and Meiszner, under the tutelage of Monsignor Swanstrom, methodically applied all the pressure the 12 Chapters could generate. The delaying tactics of Pat McCarran effectively rendered all legislative efforts temporarily useless but the political heat could still be felt. One of those closest to Swabian feelings was newly-elected Senator Paul Douglas of Illinois, who joined with Senator Myers of Pennsylvania to submit an amendment to H.R.4567 providing an appropriation of $2,500,000

> ...to pay for the transportation of such persons from Europe to the United States. The Myers-Douglas amendments would also amend the present act to make it possible for organizations to participate in the sponsorship of such persons, instead of the normal immigration procedure of individual affidavits of support.[110]

This amendment resulted directly from Douglas' attendance at a Swabian picnic that summer and would have specifically helped the *Schwobs*. In the *Chapter News* portion of the *Bulletin* under the *Doing Chicago* section, Peter Paul Reiner put it plainly enough:

> Our special guest was Senator Paul Douglas of Illinois who gave a very impressive speech and backed it up too. He promised to help us and lo and behold, the sound of the Senator's speech had hardly died down, when he and his distinguished colleague, Senator Myers of Pennsylvania introduced a bill

---

[108] Dinnerstein, *America and the Survivors*, 224.
[109] Memo to America: The DP Story, 29.
[110] 2nd Semiannual Report of the DPC, 43.

in the Senate to include our Landsleute in the same category with other nationals, so that they will also get their ocean fare paid.[111]

It is noteworthy that Senator Myers came from a state that had two large and well-organized American Aid Societies Chapters in Philadelphia and Pittsburgh.

When the Senate finally became weary of McCarran's delays and prepared to discharge the Judiciary Committee from further consideration of the bill, McCarran decided to go to Europe to undertake

...a personal survey of the displaced persons program in Europe and his findings- generally adverse to the operations- tended to prolong debate and force review of the House measure over a period of many months. Enactment waited for more than 13 months after its introduction in the House.[112]

McCarran did his best to deprecate the work of the DPC during the hearings he held and curiously, the *Schwobs* testifying during these legislative investigations actually felt that McCarran was on their side. While Nick Pesch was away in Europe on his own fact-finding mission, leadership from the Eastern *Schwobs* presented themselves to McCarran's hearings. Their report read:

Before the Senate Judiciary Committee, of which Senator McCarran is the Chairman, there appeared from our organization, the American Aid Societies, Mr. J. Wolf from Philadelphia; Mr. J. Stroebel from Elizabeth, N.J.; Mr. F. Hellman from Philadelphia and Mr. P. Yanker from N.Y.

These men gave testimony on behalf of the expellees from Roumania, Hungary and Yugoslavia. Mr. Wolf submitted a memorandum, citing facts and figures of the plight of the Donauschwaben. Mr. Yanker and Mr. Hellman spoke extemporaneously on the problem of our people and Mr. Yanker concluded, by giving the Senator the brochure.

Senators Eastland and McCarran seemed sympathetic towards our problem. In conclusion he pointed out that any legislature will have to take into consideration the unemployment situation. Sen. McCarran also emphasized that there is a great need for domestic and farm help in the U.S.A. He asked us and the other organizations that were testifying, to work out with him a bill with those facts in mind, which was done.

---

[111] A.A.S. Bulletin, September-October 1949, Vol.1, No.10.
[112] Ibid, 31.

After that we visited Sen. Langer, an oldtime friend. He was very happy to hear that we were being listened to. At last, the future seems more hopeful.[113]

These *Schwobs* had unwittingly predicted the future. In small increments the situation began to change. Lists began to appear in the *Bulletin* announcing the names of *Donauschwaben* who had finally managed to get to America. These were very short lists, in spite of the fine speeches at the Hotel Stevens. While McCarran delayed reporting to the Senate, took investigative trips to Europe, and debated the issue, the *Donauschwaben* were in their fifth year of refugee existence. Children had been born who had never known any life but that of the camps.

In his work *The Americanization of Germany*, Ralph Willett, Senior Lecturer in American Studies at the University of Hull, declared:

In the early years of the Occupation, however, the German attitude towards the American forces was still determined by the defeated nation's own wretched situation, crisply described by Melvin Lasky: '*a ruined, poverty-stricken, brutalized people, with little to eat, everything to fear, nothing to hope for*'. They were subject to curfew restrictions, could not telephone or travel any distance and were vulnerable to searches, loss of property and forced labour. In so far as the Germans were without soap, the Americans appeared spick and span; in so far as they were stripped of power, the Americans appeared strong and dominant; and perhaps above all, in so far as they were hungry and destitute, the Amis, their prosperity augmented by German servants, appeared blessed with access to a steady flow of coffee, chocolate, canned food- and most coveted of all, cigarettes. GI's enjoyed the highest daily calorie intake in the whole of Europe (4,200). The official allowance for Germans in the zone (1,550) was never reached. Even in the middle of 1948, Bavarian students protested with placards saying 'Even a dog needs 1,700 calories.' Children's essays, analyzed in *Neue Zeitung* (April 1948) were dominated by fantasies of food.[114]

The *Bulletins* of the A.A.S. during 1949 still reveal the outward-bound orientation of the relief work. In March 1949, a front-page headline involved the logistics of sending packages of food and medicine

---

[113] A.A.S. *Bulletin*, Vol.1, No.9, July-August 1949, Danube Swabian Cultural Center, Lake Villa, Illinois.
[114] Ralph Willett, *The Americanization of Germany*, (London, Routledge, 1989), 3.

to Romania through the Romanian legation in New York city. Clothing drives were big, especially in Chicago, and the New York organization mentioned two large food shipments recently sent to Vienna and Salzburg. All of the chapters were still concentrating on holding banquets, festivals, card-parties, picnics and meetings. The small numbers of refugees were easily absorbed by their grateful sponsors.

The American Aid Societies held a National Convention in New York July 3-4, 1949, and there were two pieces of good news to relate. The first was that the Internal Revenue Service had issued a proclamation on June 8, 1949, giving the A.A.S. tax-exempt status. The second bit of news was that Pesch was going to Europe to see how the organization could be bettered. Beyond these two items of positive import the general tenor of this convention is revealed in the following resolution:

DIE FLUECHTLINGSKINDER

Drawing entitled *Die Fluechtlingskinder*, artist unknown, which appeared in the December 1948 A.A.S. Bulletin

RESOLUTION

WHEREAS: There are many hundred thousand of our kinfolk among the refugees and expellees now in Germany and Austria, who are excluded from the care of the IRO because of their German ethnic origin and

WHEREAS: These people were again for that reason excluded from consideration as displaced persons by the DP Act of 1948, although they have fled or were deported from their homelands because of their religious beliefs, cultural traditions or national origin, and

WHEREAS: Discrimination on account of race, creed or nationality is inconsistent with the great and noble traditions of these United States.

THEREFORE BE IT RESOLVED: That this convention of the American Aid Societies goes on record to request our Senators to amend Public Law 774 to include those of our relatives and friends who were deported or fled from the countries of their birth because of their religious beliefs, their racial or their national origin, and

BE IT FURTHER RESOLVED: That as a means to this end, Section 12 of the Act, which gives these people a token recognition, be broadened to admit not less than 54,000 of them on the basis as other DP's, without unfair and irregular reduction of the German and Austrian quotas, in the spirit of the following amendment to correct the discrimination of sub-section (b) Section 2 of P.L. 774:
"Provided that Displaced Person shall also mean any person who otherwise complies with the requirements of Annex I of the Constitution of the IRO who solely because of his ethnic origin has been excluded from the concern of the IRO by sub-section (a) Section 4, part II of Annex I of the Constitution of the IRO.[115] [112]

The A.A.S. wasn't only battling McCarran's opposition, it also had to combat apathy among its own members. Nearly every issue of the *Bulletin* contained admonitions to the *Schwobs* to get involved, complaints that certain Chapters weren't doing what they were supposed to, and blatant attempts to create guilty consciences. Various films were shown in Chicago, films specifically designed to stimulate more interest in the relief work. One picture was even called *The Ruins of Germany*. When Pesch got back from his six-week tour of Europe, the *Bulletin* in which he describes his journey contained a sad photograph of a *Schwob* whose left leg was gone at the hip, sitting at a loom in Salzburg. The films Pesch made in Europe, while awaiting further study, reveal his attempt to portray his *Landsleute* as industrious workers. It makes for an interesting effect as *Schwobs* in Dachau are trying to look ready to work. Even more incongruous is how American they look in the clothes that had been sent to them from America.

Ironically, because of the delay created by McCarran's opposition, the tactics used to by-pass the Baltic and farm-workers preferences now backfired on the DPC. As the program neared its end, in order to be in

---

[115] A.A.S. *Bulletin*, Vol.1, No.9, July-August, 1949 Danube Swabian Cultural Center, Lake Villa, Illinois.

compliance with the numerical ratios demanded by Public Law 774, the DPC was virtually forced to admit only farmers. Furthermore, because the fight in the Senate was by no means assured, there was an administrative slow-down which accompanied the possibility that the Displaced Persons Commission would be legally terminated before the Senate reached a decision. After the slow-down there would also be an accompanying sluggish restart of operations.

The grim-faced delegates to the A.A.S. National
Convention in New York City, July 4, 1949

At the National Catholic Resettlement Conference held on March 1, 1949, at the Statler Hotel in Boston, Monsignor Swanstrom himself noted:

> While there still exists a healthy enthusiasm for the Displaced Persons program, there is to be found a definite discouragement on the part of many Catholics in the United States because of the small numbers of Displaced Persons who have presently immigrated here.[116]

---

[116] Minutes of the National Catholic Resettlement Conference, March 1, 1949, 2. Danube Swabian Cultural Center.

It would be fair to say that Nick Pesch was one of those discouraged Catholics. He attended this conference and his name appears in the minutes asking specific questions about the *Donauschwaben* who might have been overlooked in the larger scheme of overall Catholic efforts. By his presence Pesch served as a physical reminder to the NCWC that his people were Catholics as well.[117] The documents imply that the specific issue of the Swabian expellees might have been neglected were it not for his tenacity.

By Christmas of 1949, the *Schwobs* were hosting yet another Christmas banquet, this time attended by a few of those the A.A.S. had managed to rescue. Langer was of course invited, indeed at the July convention in New York he had been honored in a special letter airmailed to Washington; but when the Maverick of the Senate got to Chicago he discovered that this time he would have to share his limelight with another. The Chicago *Schwobs* had made other friends, one of whom was also an honored guest. After long years of political work the A.A.S. leadership in Chicago were taking on all the new friends they could get.

Photo courtesy American Aid Society

Photograph of war-mutilated *Schwob*
in Salzburg. A.A.S. *Bulletin*,
September-October 1949

---

[117] Ibid, 10.

Photo courtesy American Aid Society

Congressman Chester Chesney speaking at the Logan Square Masonic Temple, December 1949. The priest seated to the left of Langer is Father Ferring of St. Margaret Mary's in Chicago.

Photo courtesy American Aid Society

Senator Langer and Congressman Chesney at the banquet of the American Aid Societies, Christmas 1949, Logan Square Masonic Temple

The newcomer was Chicago-born Congressman Chester Anton Chesney, (Democrat, Illinois) a former football player for the Chicago Bears (1939-1940), who had been elected in November 1948. He was also one of those who had been at the summer picnic with Senator Paul Douglas. In the group photo shot for this occasion Chesney managed to position himself, like a football player, in the central position, seated beside a somewhat subdued-looking Bill Langer.

On November 10, 1949, the National Catholic Resettlement Council met in Columbus, Ohio, where the clergy issued a call for clothing, shoes and soap:

> Now with winter ahead, <u>unless we act at once to replenish the clothing supply</u>, many thousands of men, women and children will not be able to survive the rigors of the coming winter.[118]

Nick Pesch could hardly have been able to forget all the people he had just visited in the camps in Europe. He had toured all the major camps where *Schwobs* were housed. By this point Catholics were fairly streaming into the U.S. During fiscal year 1949 (July 1,1948- July 1,1949,) over 39,000 people would be admitted into America and another 124,164 in fiscal year 1950 (July 1,1949- June 30,1950,). Of these, forty-seven percent would be Catholics.[119] Within this group only 8,447 German expellees were included. A tiny fraction of these were *Schwobs*.

Finally, on April 5, 1950, the delays in the Senate came to an end as the vote to amend the Displaced Persons Act of 1948 culminated in a 58 to 15 victory for amendment. Just 2 weeks before the DP Act was to run out the Senate had voted to change it. Furthermore, most of the original provisions of H.R. 4567 were left in

Photo: American Aid Society

Another friend of the Chicago *Schwobs*, Senator Paul Douglas

---

[118] NCWC Resettlement Council *News Bulletin*, No.27, November 1949, 3.
[119] Memo to America: The DP Story, 78, 248.

place and virtually all of the DPC recommendations were adopted. From the Swabian point of view the entire exercise was a colossal, even criminal, waste of precious time.

Nonetheless there were victories here for them. The cut-off date was advanced to January 1,1949. The numbers were increased to 54,744. Most importantly, the technical transfer was made taking them out of the State Department's hands. These accomplishments were not overshadowed by the additional security requirements placed into the Act or the Good Faith Oath stipulation, which required that a DP swear he would abide by the terms of his sponsor's employment, under threat of deportation. As we have seen, the *Schwobs* weren't employers seeking to procure workers under the guise of humanitarianism. If they managed to get their people into the country, there was little danger that they would be discontented or disobedient.

CHAPTER NINE

PRIVATE LOYALTIES

1950 was going to be an important year for the *Schwobs* of America. They were in for more frustration, but they were also going to see results. There were numerous reasons for disappointment. The requirement for agricultural workers and Baltic Preference cases held things up right until June 1950. Then there was the cumbersome need for members of the European DPC staff to be in Washington to testify at McCarran's hearings. Furthermore, the requirements of Section 22 of the Internal Security Act, as it was being interpreted before amendment, had created a jam in the processing of refugees.

The Immigration and Nationality Act, (Public Law 414) enacted to revise the laws relating to immigration, naturalization, and nationality, also helped to clarify Section 22 of the Internal Security Act. This new law stipulated that membership in or affiliation with a totalitarian organization would not exclude people if it could be shown that their membership had been involuntary. The law now ruled that membership became involuntary if the person was under 16 years of age, if they had been inducted by action of law, or if joining up had been to get food, rations, employment or other essentials of living. In the meantime however, the old rules still applied.

The international situation added further complications. The onset of war in Korea in June of 1950, caused the U.S. Army to take over DP camps in every part of Germany, dispersing the refugees and making processing even more difficult. Some DPC personnel, possibly concerned that the Reds might invade Europe, resigned and came home, some to join the military. This left the DPC with a vacuum which practically stopped the movement of refugees. There was also new red tape created by the amendments to the DP Act. The Chief Historian of the DPC commented:

The 1950 amendments to the Act required the promulgation of new regulations and their implementation by new procedures- for example, the "good faith" oath made necessary the establishment of new procedures which required time to initiate and to perfect. Section 13, as amended, lengthened the security processing. Cases had to be reinvestigated, new reports written, and the process became longer and more time consuming.[120]

As if these difficulties weren't enough, on September 1, 1950, the British Army took away facilities it had allowed the DPC to use, forcing the DPC to hire and train even more staff. Then the ships earmarked for refugee transport were withdrawn. They would be needed for Korea. The DPC now had to have a Congressional appropriation to use funds to pay the IRO for use of their facilities and ships. It would take Congress until September 27, 1950, to authorize that money.

Lastly, in a most maddening development, the United States High Commissioner for Germany and the Bonn Government

...insisted that Bonn Government facilities be used instead of those of the IRO. Although the Commission had already perfected complete arrangements and despite the obvious delay that would result, it acceded to the High Commissioner's request because of the interests which such request would serve. The Bonn Government, it was agreed, would provide housing and other physical care including immunization. The IRO processing centers would be used for the United States Public Health Service examination, the execution of the "good faith" oath, the issuance of immigration visas, and the preexamination by the Immigration and Naturalization Service. The Bonn Government further agreed to prepare documentation for German expellees and to provide transportation of expellees to centers and to the port of embarkation. ...The Bonn Government was slow in providing facilities and personnel for documentation. The Bonn Government agreed to provide the holding centers by October 15,1950. In late November only one holding center in the vicinity of Bremen was made available and this one proved to be of no use to the operation. By December 31, 1950, neither personnel nor facilities had been made available by the Bonn Government anywhere in Germany.[121]

By contrast, the Austrians immediately made centers available in Salzburg and thus the only visas issued to German expellees in 1950 were issued in Austria. By July of 1951, admissions of German expellees would amount to 2,040, or roughly one quarter of the 8,447 expellees

---

[120] Memo to America: The DP Story, 82.
[121] Ibid, 85.

who had come by June of 1950. In the very midst of an immigrant monsoon, the German expellees were experiencing drought.

As usual, the largest part of the problem lay in red-tape. All of the original affidavits submitted under the Displaced Persons Act were now invalid. They had to be re-submitted as assurances under the amended law. The *Donauschwaben,* who had by now become experts in the tedious processes of paperwork in triplicate, handled the changes with dispatch. The lists in the *Bulletin* began to grow longer. By the end of the year the *Schwobs* began to see hope for their people. The A.A.S. Bulletin of November 1950, observed:

> This office has been a beehive of activity. Since the new law went into effect in July, providing FREE overseas transportation for our *Landsleute* in Germany and Austria, IF Job and Housing Assurance is given, thousands of such forms were sent to all our chapters.[122]

Up to this point all the names of recent arrivals published in the *Bulletin* were accompanied by the proud listing of those that had sponsored them. These were overwhelmingly family-related. Now the situation took on a new dimension. Suddenly the *Schwobs* of America were in a position to bring absolute strangers over, simply through the expedient of the NCWC's blanket assurances.

This presented the *Schwobs* with a real chance to test their *Landsleute* rhetoric against reality. The long years of investigation, documentation and processing had produced a surplus of expellee cases waiting for assurances. It was as if the *Schwobs* had been watching a high-wire act for years, a show during which Nick Pesch climbed up on a bicycle and John Meiszner got on his shoulders and the pair of them went riding down a cable strung between wind-swept legislative skyscrapers. The *Schwobs* had watched this drama for years and they could hope that one day all their efforts would produce results. Now it had.

Suddenly they were put in the position to get up on that bicycle and climb onto Nick Pesch's shoulders, a clear difference between theory and practice. Sponsoring a long-lost brother or sister (or even an in-law) was

---

[122] A.A.S. *Bulletin,* Vol.2, No. 2, November 1950.

one thing. Sponsoring an unknown *Schwob*, merely because he was a *Schwabenkind*, was a real test of convictions. Helen Meiszner explained that

> ...some people thought that these men were crazy...doing all of this...people that they didn't know from a barrel of hay...and all...and to sponsor them and sign on the dotted line to the government and all. So a lot of them thought Pesch and Meiszner had holes in their head for doing that, but they felt strongly about it, and wanted to be humanitarians and do what they could for these people...[123]

Richard Gunther was one of those who signed on the dotted line, without his parents' knowledge. He remembers:

> We'd have our meetings, and so on, and now we have these applications and so on and who's going to sign them? Now everyone who signed, now that was a big undertaking. We did not know these people out there. You may have known Uncle Fritz or you may have known Aunt Katy...but you did not know the people in general. We had no idea, are they good...are they bad, or what. All we knew was that they were *Schwobs*...
>
> John Meiszner signed for oodles of them, I can't tell you how many. If at the end of a meeting there was still a stack [of applications] an inch thick, or whatever was left, you could always guarantee Peter Paul Reiner would sign for whatever was left...[124]

The *Schwobs* were understandably proud of their courage to sign blanket assurances and felt slighted when their contributions were overlooked. Helen Meiszner recalled the time when John Meiszner came home and announced that he and Pesch had signed for 300 families. In late January 1951, someone, probably John Meiszner, scribbled a petulant note and attached it to the official minutes of the Diocesan Resettlement Directors meeting, which had been held at the Hotel Sherman in Chicago on January 22, 1951. On page 9 of these minutes the Catholic hierarchy listed those dioceses which had submitted blanket assurances. Chicago was conspicuously missing. The complaint read:

> Chicago- American Aid Societies sent Blanket Assurances for 200 families to Father Doyle on December 15, 1950. Why is there no mention of that?[125]

---

[123] Helen Meiszner, taped interview with author, June 1997.

[124] Richard Gunther, interview with author, May 1997.

[125] Handwritten note attached to official minutes of Diocesan Resettlement Directors Meeting, Chicago, January 22, 1951. Source: American Aid Society.

At the National Catholic Resettlement Council meeting held at the Hotel Vanderbilt in New York City on April 12, 1951, Nick Pesch could still be found fighting for his people. The secretary recorded the following exchange:

> Mr. Pesch of the American Aid Society expressed a wish to clarify a point. In a communication he received it was pointed out that we are trying to extend the Displaced Persons Act as to the cut-off date. He wondered if Germans were also considered in this. There is hardly a family where someone is not affected in one way or another as a result of the cut-off date. He explained there would be a much better chance to get families together if the cut-off date were extended for German ethnics, as well as displaced persons.
> Monsignor Swanstrom explained that we had intended, if we said anything about the cut-off date, to extend cut-off date for ethnic group as well.[126]

Swanstrom apparently did not take Pesch and the A.A.S. lightly. The very next day, April 13, 1951, he sent Pesch a list of 76 organizations which the Committee on Internal Security of the DPC had removed from its 'Secret List'. This was a compilation of organizations which the DPC initially ruled as being automatic grounds for exclusion for a visa. Swanstrom sent Pesch a copy of this confidential document, which was clearly marked by the DPC in red as being 'For Staff Use Only - No Public Release'. Swanstrom undoubtedly had access to this kind of information through Edward O'Connor. Pesch was included in the loop as well.

At this conference the Catholics discussed, as usual, their best strategies with regard to Congress. They related geo-political and economic realities in Europe and elsewhere with the candor of those who hold genuine authority and brought up items such as how best to circumvent organized labor's opposition to liberalized immigration laws. Swanstrom further explained that the DPC would no longer exclude applicants automatically, merely on the basis of membership in one of the organizations on its 'Secret List', unless they had held office in one of these organizations and could therefore be considered 'active Nazis'.

---

[126] Official Minutes, National Catholic Resettlement Council, New York, N.Y., April 12,1951, 6. Danube Swabian Cultural Center.

WAR RELIEF SERVICES — NATIONAL CATHOLIC WELFARE CONFERENCE
350 FIFTH AVENUE
NEW YORK 1, N. Y.

NATIONAL HEADQUARTERS:
1312 Massachusetts Ave., N. W.
Washington, D. C.

Telephone :
Wisconsin 7-8586

April 13, 1951

Mr. Nick Pesch
American Aid Societies
1220 North Bosworth Ave.
Chicago 22, Illinois

Dear Mr. Pesch:

In accordance with my promise, I am enclosing a copy of the list of organizations removed from the D.P.C. secret list.

I will follow through on the other matters we talked about yesterday.

It was good to see you again.

With every best wish, I am

Sincerely yours,

(Rt. Rev. Msgr.) Edward E. Swanstrom
Executive Director

EES/CD
Enclosure

Photo courtesy American Aid Society. A.A.S. Records, Danube Swabian Cultural Center, Lake Villa, Illinois

Monsignor Swanstrom's letter to Nick Pesch in which
he enclosed a confidential list, April 13, 1951

Swanstrom explained that now cases would be

...examined in the light of the liberal interpretation of the Internal Security Act and revised regulations on Section 13 of the Displaced Persons Act.[127]

At the Christmas banquet of 1950 the *Schwobs* of America were looking at a changed political landscape. Their people were coming in faster than ever and they were an integral part of the operation through the NCWC's blanket assurance capability. In keeping with these changes new faces appeared at the Logan Square Masonic Temple. Monsignor Swanstrom himself was in attendance, a reasonable sign of the growing importance of the A.A.S. within the Catholic sphere. Congressman Timothy P. Sheehan of Illinois' Eleventh District was present. There was also a personal friend of John Meiszner at the table for honored guests. His name was Everett McKinley Dirksen, and he was a brand new U.S. Senator.

Photo courtesy Helen Meiszner

Everett McKinley Dirksen with John Meiszner at the Logan Square Masonic Temple, December 10, 1950.

It is fair to say that Ev Dirksen had been helped into the Senate by John Meiszner, who worked diligently to deliver votes through the German-American Committee For Dirksen, and the Honorable Mr. Marigold never forgot it. Helen Meiszner claims that Dirksen served as John Meiszner's personal role model.[128] Just how much Meiszner aided the Senator is evident from the way Dirksen reciprocated, especially during the second wave of refugees to come beginning in 1953.[129] Later, when Dirksen's notorious 'flexibility' garnered him patronage influence from Democratic Presidents, he would repay Meiszner by making

---

[127] Ibid, 17.
[128] Helen Meiszner, interview with author, May 1997.
[129] This second wave awaits further study.

him the U.S. Marshal for the Northern District of Illinois and a Collector of Customs. For now however, he was just happy to attend John Meiszner's favorite charity banquet at the Logan Square Masonic Temple.

It may be assumed that Dirksen, who was of German origin, also shared some *mitgefühl* with John Meiszner's *Schwobs*. Although Bill Langer endeared himself to the Schwobs by speaking to them in German,[130] Dirksen's rural roots in downstate Illinois gave him an 'almost' Swabian background. Edward and Frederick Schapsmeier record that:

> Near the turn of the century the north side of Pekin acquired the appellation of 'Beantown'. This name came from the large number of bean patches cultivated by the residents of this particular area of town, heavily populated by German immigrants and semirural in nature. Beantown, or 'Bohnchefiddle' in the Low German vernacular of its inhabitants, was dotted with white frame houses, each adjacent to a sizable garden. Those living in this locale were of lower economic status than others in Pekin, yet the neat appearance of the homes belied this fact. Beantown may have been the so-called poor end of town, but in no way was it a slum or a run-down section of Pekin.
>
> It was into this particular political, social, and economic milieu that Everett McKinley Dirksen would be born and raised. His parents, Johann and Antje, were both German immigrants.[131]

---

[130] Richard Gunther interview with author, May 1997.

[131] Edward L. Schapsmeier, Frederick H. Schapsmeier, *Dirksen of Illinois: Senatorial Statesman*, (Urbana, Chicago, University of Illinois Press, 1985), 2.

Photo courtesy Helen Meiszner

Senator Dirksen pressing the flesh at the Logan Square Masonic
Temple while John Meiszner looks on, December 10,1950

Photo courtesy American Aid Society

Ev Dirksen singing with the Schwobs in 1954

Photo courtesy American Aid Society

Dirksen speaking at the Logan Square Masonic Temple
December 10,1950

Photo courtesy Helen Meiszner

Senator Dirksen with a pair of Swabian girls in traditional costume

Photo courtesy Helen Meiszner
Group photo at Logan Square Masonic Temple, December 10, 1950

Photo courtesy Helen Meiszner
John Meiszner as U.S. Collector of Customs, showing
display to Miss U.S. Customs, his daughter Joyce Meiszner

Photo courtesy Helen Meiszner

John Meiszner inspecting his troops

The *Schwobs* of America, with Nick Pesch and John Meiszner as their leaders, had chiseled out for themselves a tiny hole in the imposing barrier of U.S. immigration. Through that small opening almost 54,000 people would find America. There was good reason for the smiles at the 1950 banquet. The Great Rescue was coming.

CHAPTER TEN

THE GREAT RESCUE

When the Great Rescue finally happened for the expellees it was clear the Pipeline had suddenly burst open. Compared with the previous year, which saw 2,040 German expellees trickle through, this was a virtual flood of people. Between July 1st, 1951, and the end of the program on June 30th, 1952, just twelve short months, a total of 42,796 German expellees got off transport ships in New York and New Orleans. When the Pipeline was legally clamped shut on June 30th there were approximately 50,000 expellees left stuck in it. The DPC estimated that 32,000 of those would have been eligible to be admitted.[132]

By this time the *Schwobs* of Chicago, St. Louis, Milwaukee, Buffalo, the Bronx, Philadelphia, Pittsburgh, Detroit, Cincinnati, Mansfield, and Elizabeth N.J. were ready to absorb their people from Europe. Like some incredible social sponge the refugees were taken in as soon as they arrived, sucked into American society by sponsors who had been preparing for their arrival for years. This rescue deserves the label 'great' precisely because it was accomplished in such mundane fashion by such ordinary people. There were no Rockefellers among the *Schwobs* to underwrite their rescue. They did it by themselves.

The *Schwobs* in Chicago had amassed hundreds of places to put their refugees. Privately owned apartments, rooming houses and homes in every part of the city and suburbs were used. The work of co-ordinating all these dwellings was almost as amazing as the network of employers the *Donauschwaben* had created. From large factories down to the smallest businesses, Chicago willingly accepted Swabian workers, whose reputations had preceded them. The Dormeyer Appliance Company and Florsheim Shoes were at one end of the spectrum while at the other was a farmer in Arlington Heights who had a spare house on

---

[132] Memo to America: The DP Story, 86.

his land and would let refugees set up a 'truck garden' if they wanted to.[133]

The list of employers cuts across every conceivable occupation, but the *Schwobs* claim that janitors played a pivotal role in the Swabian socio-economic picture. Because it was an ideal occupation for them, many Swabian immigrants to Chicago after World War I joined the Janitor's Union. It was perfect for their needs in a variety of ways. Probably foremost was the lack of any requirement to immediately learn English in order to work. In the hallways and empty rooms there was no need for social discourse, and even those with the most rudimentary English could understand what a supervisor meant when he pointed to the mop, the floor buffer or the toilet brush. The *Schwobs* had a proud, pioneering heritage but they had come to America to work and to build, and they were taking anything they could get.

A second benefit was that janitors operated largely during the graveyard shift, freeing them up during the daytime to take a second job or work on their property. It became almost a standard Swabian practice to buy and fix up a home or a two-flat. The formula seemed to be: buy a two-flat, put it in order, sell it and buy a four-flat, then a six-flat, and finally an apartment building. If the *Schwobs* were strongly represented in the Janitor's Union, they were an even more potent force in the Chicago real estate market. A study of the Affidavits of Support issued under the initial DP Act, and the Job and the Housing Assurances required by the amended Act reveals the astonishing number of property owners among the *Schwobs*. Some owned 2 or 3 apartment buildings while listing their employment as auto mechanics, brick masons, painters, bakers, barbers, knitters, dyers, janitors, and widowed housewives. Because of the intrusive nature of the Affidavit of Support, the *Schwobs* were forced to reveal their financial status. While the amount of wealth listed was never very great, real estate, usually rental property, was found on most of the statements.[134]

---

[133] Assurances folder, A.A.S. Records, Danube Swabian Cultural Center, Lake Villa, Illinois.
[134] Assurances folder, A.A.S. Records, Danube Swabian Cultural Center, Lake Villa, Illinois.

The arrival of refugees at Union Depot, circa 1952.

Volksdeutsche by the Dozen

From behind the Iron Curtain to resettlement on an Ohio farm is the story of the 12-member Webel family, which came to this country Monday, March 19, under the amended Displaced Persons Act.

Following their arrival in New York by plane, Mr. and Mrs. Jakob Webel, left that morning by train for Medina, Ohio, and a reunion with Mr. Webel's sister and her husband, Mr. and Mrs. Jakob Keiper, residents of Medina for the past 30 years.

The Keipers, who sponsored the immigration of the Webels under the DP Act, built a house for them three years ago.

The Webel's are "Expellees," so-called because they are people of Germanic origin who were forced to flee from Eastern Europe by the Communists. Under the amended Displaced Persons Act, 54,744 expellees are eligible for visas by June 30, 1952.

The Webels were forced to leave their native Yugoslavia late in the war. Until the War's close, they drifted from Silesia to Czechoslovakia and Bavaria. The present regime in Yugoslavia prevented them from returning home and they settled down on an Austrian farm, waiting for a chance to come to the United States.

The ten children range in age from 16-year-old Reinhardt to Daniel, age three months. In the picture, left to right, are: First row—Jacob, 4; Rosalia, 6; Theresia, 10; Robert, 8. Second row—Karl, 13; Elisabeth, 15; Adolf, 12; Katherina (in her father's arms) 2; Mr. Webel. Third row—Reinhardt, 17; John W. Gibson, Chairman of the Displaced Persons Commissions, Mrs. Webel holding Daniel, 2 months old.

Photo courtesy American Aid Society

John W. Gibson and expellees of German ethnic origin.
Reported in German weekly newspaper, *Eintracht*, June 1951

This may be partly because during this last, flood-stage year when refugees were pouring in, the *Schwobs* had to find all kinds of ingenious methods to guarantee someone a job or a place to live. This may explain why homes suddenly became 'two flats' and cleaning ladies had room for 'domestic servants'. There were also many men and women who had become related to *Schwobs* by marriage and who were compelled by love to help their spouse's relatives. However it was managed, the *fait accompli* remains.

There are 479 arrival envelopes still left among the A.A.S. cache of documents, and witnesses say that the arrivals were at least quadruple that, so the Chicago total for 1951-52 would be around 2,000. To this number must be added the hundreds of private assurances that the A.A.S. helped its members fill out and follow up on.[135]

Whatever the numbers, volunteers were needed for the task of meeting the trains at Union Depot. After years of selling raffle tickets and sending packages to hungry people in Europe, it was a rewarding duty. In New York and New Orleans the refugees were given large manila envelopes by the War Relief Services Division of the NCWC. On the back there were instructions in four languages. They were to keep their train tickets and schedules in these envelopes, which they did, as attested by the fact that they remained still neatly placed there over fifty years later.[136] They were told to wear their WRS-NCWC buttons on their clothing so they could be easily identified by those who were picking them up at their destination. As the photo on page 103 attests, they stood in the great maw of Union Depot like children wearing name tags on their first day of school, looking conspicuous, waiting for someone to take them by the hand.

---

[135] Ibid.
[136] Ibid.

Photo courtesy American Aid Society

Rescued Donauschwaben, circa 1952

Photo courtesy American Aid Society

Nick Pesch and his people, circa 1952

Someone was always there. After arrival they were usually transported to the Social Turner Hall at 1653 Belmont Avenue, where they could gather their wits. It must have been here that they finally understood that they were safe. They were among their *Landsleute*. The Aid Society then immediately saw to it that the refugees were fed by Al Wirth, who ran a small restaurant and bar on the first floor of the Hall.[137]

Unlike refugees sponsored by individuals who knew them, these people were strangers. There were many difficulties inherent in such a situation. Richard Gunther simply said: 'Nothing was easy' and mentioned as an example the situation whereby miscommunications sometimes resulted in one family receiving an apartment that was large enough to hold a bigger one. When this family would then have to be moved to make room for the newcomers, it was understandably problematic.[138]

Another kind of trouble was related to the refugees' perceptions of the American Aid Society. The political pretensions of the A.A.S. were partly responsible for this. In the effort to influence legislators the A.A.S. naturally played themselves up. The refugees in Europe could not help seeing the A.A.S. via the image they had created to impress the Congress. To the refugee in a DP camp the A.A.S. looked like a powerful organization. This was, of course, largely an illusion. When the refugees arrived and discovered that the President of the American Aid Societies was a poor tailor, that the National Secretary ran a modest funeral home, and that the Corporate Office was really in a hair products factory, there was some disbelief and disillusionment. Helen Meiszner tells how many of these refugees expected Meiszner and Pesch to be like the wealthy barons they had known in the old country, some even hoping to work on their estates.

Yet these misunderstandings do not diminish The Great Rescue. Quite the contrary, the effort made by many unsung individuals was immense. A woman named Mary Lazich for example, officially sponsored 82 persons. A woman who worked in the Corporate Office of the A.A.S., Michela Simak, personally signed for 31 people when

---

[137] Helen Meiszner, taped interview with author, May 1997.
[138] Richard Gunther taped interview with author, May 1996.

sponsors could not be found in time. Even Nick Pesch, poor man that he was, put his name down for 13 people.[139]

The work with the refugees was labor and time-intensive. They had to be brought into the great tumult of Chicago, a process which worked itself out in hundreds of mundane and yet vital ways. Their children had to be registered for school, paperwork had to be filled out in many different offices, jobs had to be reached, employers met, bus routes shown, English taught. The Great Rescue unfolded within the commonplace things of life, superimposing sensational events onto simple ones. They managed it well and without fanfare. Refugees who had walked from Rumania, Hungary and Yugoslavia all the way to Austria or Germany would find the Chicago bus system something of a luxury.

Photo courtesy Helen Meiszner

The *Schwobs* celebrating Christmas at
the Social Turner Hall, December 1951

Christmas in America, above and on the next page:

---

[139] Based on author's count of assurances found with Nick Pesch's signature on them, A.A.S. Records, Assurances Folder, Danube Swabian Cultural Center.

Photo courtesy Helen Meiszner

John Meiszner's daughter, Joyce, distributing gifts to refugee children.

The Schwobs who came and those who brought them never really said a public word about their Great Rescue. They never tried to publish any account of it. Rather, they packed all the documents into boxes and left them alone. It was Joe Stein who found them, many years later, molding away in a barn on their Lake Villa property. He rescued them in the nick of time for the barn was about to be torn down.

After November 1950, there were no more issues of the A.A.S. *Bulletin.* Joe Stein explained that they were too busy with people to worry about publishing the periodical. This is eloquent evidence that the *Schwobs* had what they really wanted. Shrugging off their incredible hardships, they went about the business of life in America.

The title of this book, *The Great Chicago Refugee Rescue*, was chosen precisely because of the contrast between who the American *Schwobs* were and what they accomplished. It is this contrast which urges me to argue that this event qualifies as both a rescue and a great one. Using the vehicle of American politics, the little people had managed a magnificent feat.

Photo courtesy American Aid Society

A pair of Swabian girls, probably sisters, rescued from the camps

Nick Pesch and John Meiszner weren't through by June 1952. For the next five years, as the Communists began clamping down hard on Eastern Europe, the *Schwobs* continued to agitate on Capitol Hill to get more of their people out under The Refugee Relief Act of 1953. Swabian witnesses claim that eventually close to 17,000 refugees were signed for by the American Aid Society in Chicago alone.[140] It was largely the German *Wirtschaftswunder* that weakened the pull of America for Swabian refugees and ended the Great Rescue, but for a while they had a noble and compassionate cause. Pesch, Meiszner and those working with them have deservedly become heroes to the small group of people that they saved.

---

[140] According to Joe Stein, Hans Gebavi, Richard Gunther and others. Full statistics and tabulations await further study.

EPILOGUE

In some ways the Great Rescue has been somewhat of a mixed blessing. In the solvent of American freedom the social cement that bound the *Schwobs* together has been weakening. The next generation of *Schwobs* have lived an existence new in Swabian history. They have had none of the disaster and death that molded their forefathers into a special people, none of the enemies that kept them cohesive, none of the hunger and deprivation that made them wise and frugal.

Photo: author

Wreath-laying at the Nick Pesch Memorial, 1996

Some of the faithful children still attend the annual memorial services for the *Donauschwaben* dead, laying wreaths and death-camp crosses at the foot of the Nick Pesch Memorial in Lake Villa, but they are few. It is mostly the old ones who come. It is difficult for American children to experience vicariously the horrors their parents and grand-parents had to endure. One Swabian woman tells the story of how she was taken to a slave labor camp in Russia after the war and insists that for 17 months she existed in a mine where her legs were constantly in water almost up to her knees. Such suffering is unimaginable to most American-born children.

Photo: author

> The death-camp crosses of the *Donauschwaben*, Memorial Day, 1997. Each name represents a Swabian village turned into a *Vernichtungslager* for *Schwobs* after the war.

The A.A.S. today is struggling to keep the *Schwobs* of America from melting away in America's affluence. Unlike the powerfully cohesive group of refugees who went to Brazil and worked the same kind of miracle their forefathers did in the old Austro-Hungarian Empire, the *Schwobs* in the United States splintered into many sub-groups.

The children born in America are naturally somewhat distant from the suffering of their parents and grandparents. In a sense the American *Donauschwaben* are paying the price of peace and prosperity.

This is not to say that they are dying out, as a people or as an organization. In fact, as this thesis is being written the *Schwobs* are supervising the construction of a large new building at their Lake Villa compound and there is talk of healing the rifts which occurred after the Great Rescue. In the end, I hope, they will remain united and loyal to one another. The force of a stream is not diminished by the obstacles it encounters, indeed, the purest water may actually be that which has driven a path through solid stone.

Professor Barber once told me that the 'twentieth century is unintelligible without George Orwell'. If, as Orwell claimed, concentration camps form 'part of the pattern of our time', then let rescuers also be a part of that pattern.[141]

Photo: author

The German Hungarian Old People's Home,
now the Cultural Center of the Danube-Swabians, 1997.

---

[141] George Orwell, *Collected Essays, Journalism and Letters*, Vol.IV, p.421, Letter to Roger Senhouse, May,1948.

*They were not loyal to a party or a country or an idea,
they were loyal to one another.*

Nick Fritz of Romania (l) with his friend Peter Krebs of Hungary (r)

SELECTED BIBLIOGRAPHY

Anabring, Matthias. *Volksgeschichte der Deutschen in Ungarn*. Stuttgart: Verlag Südost Stimmen, 1954.

Barber, Charles M. "Nordamerikanischer Sängerbund versus The U.S. Treasury Department, 1944-46." *Yearbook of German-American Studies*, Vol. 30, (1995), 73-116.

_____. "The Expulsion of Germans from East Central Europe: The Ethnic German Danube-Swabians from East Central Europe, 1944-48".

Unpublished paper presented at Northern Great Plains History Conference, Sioux Falls, South Dakota, October 15,1987.

_____. "Vertreibungsbibliographie and the Work of Alfred M. de Zayas".

Unpublished paper presented at The Eleventh Annual Symposium of the Society for German-American Studies, April 25, 1987.

_____. "Rejected Pioneers: The Danube-Swabians Between Balkan Nationalism and National Socialism, 1918-1941". Unpublished paper.

_____. "Nazis and Anti-Nazis among the Volksdeutsche of East Central Europe, 1933-1945". Unpublished paper presented at the 28th Northern Great Plains History Conference, Pierre, South Dakota, October 1993.

_____. "Senator Langer and German-American Opposition to the Morganthau Plan". Unpublished paper.

_____. "Senator William Langer and the Volksdeutsche, 1944-49". Unpublished paper presented at 26th Annual Northern Great Plains History Conference, Mankato, Minnesota, October 3, 1991.

_____. "Senator Langer's Isolationism and the Fate of Germans, 1944-1954". Unpublished paper presented at 27th Annual Northern Great Plains History Conference, Fargo, North Dakota, October 3,1992.

Beer, Josef. *Donauschwäbische Zeitgeschichte Aus Erster Hand*. Donauschwäbisches Archiv, Reihe III/Band 38 D-7032 Sindelfingen, Goldmuhlestr. 30, Haus Der Donauschwaben. München: 1987.

Benda, Julien. *The Treason of the Intellectuals (La Trahison des Clercs).* New York: William Morrow, 1928.

Bischoff, Ralph F. *Nazi Conquest through German Culture.* Cambridge: Harvard University Press, 1942.

Borsky, G. *The Enemy Within: German Minorities as a Weapon of German Policy.* London: Hutchinson and Co., 1943.

Bresser, Michael. *The Danube-Swabians: Biography of a People from Inception to Dispersal.* Philadelphia: Danube-Swabian Association, 1277 Southampton Road, Philadelphia, PA. 19116.

Braubach, Max. *Prinz Eugen von Savoyen. Eine Biographie.* Vol.I (1963); *Aufstieg*; Vol.II(1964), *Der Feldherr*; Vol.III (1964), *Zum Geipfel des Ruhmes*; Vol. IV (1965), *Der Staatsmann*; Vol.V (1965), *Mensch und Schicksal*, (Vienna, Verlag für Geschichte und Politik.)

Carinthiacus. *The Position of the Slovenes under Austria Compared with that of the German Minority in the Serb, Croat, Slovene Kingdom.* Ljublana: National Minorities Institute, 1925.

Clay, Lucius D. *Decision in Germany.* New York: 1950.

Craig, Gordon A. "The Compleat Feldherr". *Central European History*, December (1968).

_____. *The Germans.* New York: Penguin Books USA Inc., 1991.

Davidson, Eugene. *The Death and Life of Germany: An Account of the American Occupation.* Urbana: University of Illinois Press.

Dawson, W.H. *The German Empire 1867-1914 and the Unity Movement.* New York: Macmillan, 1919.

de Zayas, Alfred M. *Nemesis at Potsdam, The Anglo-Americans and the Expulsion of the Germans.* London: Routledge, 1977.

_____. *The Wehrmacht War Crimes Bureau, 1939-1945.* Lincoln, Nebraska: University of Nebraska Press, 1989.

_____. *A Terrible Revenge: The Ethnic Cleansing of the East European Germans, 1944-1950.* New York: St. Martin's Press, 1994.

Dinnerstein, Leonard. *America and the Survivors of the Holocaust.* New York: Columbia University Press, 1982.

Djilas, Milovan. *Memoir of a Revolutionary.* New York: Harcourt Brace, 1973.

Douglas, Paul II. *In the Fullness of Time: The Memoirs of Paul H. Douglas.* New York: Harcourt Brace Jovanovich, Inc., 1971.

Drury, Allen. *A Senate Journal, 1943-1945.* New York: McGraw-Hill Inc., 1963.

Egger, Leopold. *Das Vermögen und Die Vermögensverluste Der Deutschen in Jugoslawien.* Sindelfingen: Landsmannschaft Der Donauschwaben, 1983.

Engelmann, Nikolaus. *The Banat Germans.* Translated by John M. Michels, Reprinted 1987 with permission of Pannonia Verlag, D-8228 Freilassing/ Bayern (1966), by the University of Mary Press, Bismarck, North Dakota.

Feingold, Henry L. *The Politics of Rescue.* New Brunswick: Rutgers University Press, 1970.

Fleischhauer, Ingeborg, and Benjamin Pinkus. *The Soviet Germans, Past and Present.* New York: St. Martin's Press, 1986.

Gruber, Wendelin. Translated by Frank Schmidt. *In The Claws Of The Red Dragon: Ten Years Under Tito's Heel.* Toronto: St. Michaelswerk Pub., 1988.

Hofmeister, Rudolph A. *The Germans of Chicago.* Champaign, Illinois: Stipes Pub. Co., 1976.

Holli, Melvin G. and Peter d'A. Jones, ed. *Ethnic Chicago: A Multicultural Portrait.* Grand Rapids, Mich., Wm. B. Eerdmans Pub. Co., 1995.

Jaszi, Oscar. *The Dissolution of the Hapsburg Monarchy.* Chicago: 1929.

Janko, Sepp. *Weg und Ende der deutschen Volksgruppe in Jugoslawien.* 2. Auflage, Graz-Stuttgart: Leopold Stocker Verlag, 1983.

Kallay, Nicholas. *Hungarian Premier: A Personal Account of a Nation's Struggle in the Second World War.* New York: Columbia University Press, 1954.

Kallbrunner, Josef. *Das Kaiserliche Banat I, Einrichtung und Entwicklung des Banats bis 1739.* München: Verlag des Südostdeutschen Kulturwerks, 1958.

Kann, Robert A. *The Peoples of the Eastern Habsburg Lands, 1526-1918. A History of East Central Europe, Vol. VI.,* Seattle: University of Washington Press, 1984.

Kennan, George F. *Memoirs 1925-1950.* Boston: Little, Brown and Co., 1967.

Kertesz, Stephen. "Soviet and Western Policies in Hungary 1944-1947." *The Review of Politics, XIV, No.1.*

_____. "The Expulsion of the Germans from Hungary: A Study in Postwar Diplomacy", *The Review of Politics, XV, No.2,* Notre Dame, Indiana.

_____. *Between Russia and the West: Hungary and the Illusions of Peacemaking, 1945-1947.* Notre Dame, Indiana: University of Notre Dame Press, 1984.

Koehl, Robert L. *RKFDV, German Resettlement and Population Policy, 1939-1945, A History of the Reich Commission for the Strengthening of Germandom.* Cambridge: Harvard University Press, 1957.

_____. *The Black Corps, The Structure and Power Struggles of the Nazi SS.* Madison: University of Wisconsin Press, 1983.

Koehler, Eve Eckert. *Seven Susannahs: Daughters of the Danube.* Milwaukee, Wis.: Schmidt Bros. Printing Co. Inc.,1976.

_____. *Who Are The Donauschwaben?* Milwaukee, Wis.: privately printed, 1988.

_____. *The Danube Germans.* Milwaukee, Wis.: privately printed, 1988.

_____. "Volga Germans, Danube Germans: Your People Are My People". *The Journal of the American Historical Society of Germans from Russia,* Fall 1988, Vol. 11, No. 3, pps. 30-33.

Komjathy, Anthony and Rebecca Stockwell. *German Minorities and the Third Reich.* New York: Holmes & Meier Pub. Inc.,1980.

Leicht Sebastion. *Weg der Donauschwaben.* Passau: Verlag Passavia Passau, 1983.

Long, James. *The German-Russians: A Bibliography of Russian Materials.* Oxford: Clio Books, 1978.

_____. *From Privlileged to Dispossessed: The Volga Germans, 1860-1917.* Lincoln: University of Nebraska Press, 1988.

Luebke, Frederick. *Bonds of Loyalty.* Northern Illinois University Press, 1974.

Lumans, Valdis O. *Himmler's Auxiliaries: The Volksdeutsche Mittelstelle and the German National Minorities of Europe 1933-1945.* Chapel Hill: University of North Carolina Press, 1993.

Luža, Radomír. *The Transfer of the Sudeten Germans: A Study of Czech-German Relations 1933-1962.* New York: New York University Press, 1964.

MaCartney, C.A. *Hungary and Her Successors: The Treaty of Trianon and its Consequences 1919-1937.* London: Oxford University Press, 1937.

_____. with A.W. Palmer. *Independent Eastern Europe*. New York: St. Martin's Press, 1966.

_____. *Hungary: A Short History*. London: Cambridge University Press.

_____. *Problems of the Danube Basin*. Cambridge: Harvard University Press.

_____. *A History of Hungary, 1929-1945*. New York: Praeger, 1957.

MacNeil, Neil. *Dirksen: Portrait of a Public Man*. New York: The World Pub. Co., 1970.

McNeill, William H. *Europe's Steppe Frontier 1500-1800*. Chicago: University of Chicago Press, 1964.

Montgomery, John F. *Hungary The Unwilling Satellite*. New York: The Devin-Adair Co. 1947.

Müller-Guttenbrunn, Adam. *Der Grosse Schwabenzug*. Sersheim: Oswald Hartmann Verlag, 1990.

Müller-Wlossak, Traudie. *Die Peitsche des Tito-Kommissars*. Passau: Passavia Druckerei GmbH, 1987.

Nagelbach, Michael A. *Heil! And Farewell: A Life in Romania, 1913-1946*. Chicago: Adams Press, 1986.

O'Connor, Len. *Clout: Mayor Daley and His City*. Chicago: Henry Regnery Co., 1975.

Orwell, George. *A Collection of Essays*. New York: Harcourt Brace & Co., 1981.

_____. *1984*. Harcourt Brace Jovanovich, 1949.

Paikert, Geza C. *The Danube Swabians: German Populations in Hungary, Rumania and Yugoslavia and Hitler's Impact on their Patterns*. The Hague: Martinus Nijhoff, 1967.

_____. *The German Exodus, A Selective Study on the Post-War Expulsion of German Populations and its Effects*. The Hague: Martinus Nijhoff, 1962.

Petersen, Carl and others. *Handwörterbuch des Grenz und Auslanddeutschtums*. Breslau: Ferdinand Hirt, 1936.

Rasimus, Hans. *Als Fremde Im Vaterland*. München: Donauschwäbisches Archiv, 1989.

Reichling, G. *Die Heimatsvertriebenen im Spiegel der Statistik*. Berlin: Verlag von Duncker Humblot, 1958.

Reining, Conrad C. "The Rise and Demise of the German Minority in Hungary". *Folia Slavica*, Vol. 1, No. 3, 'Sociolinguistic Problems in Czechoslovakia, Hungary, Romania and Yugoslavia', ed. William R. Schmalstieg and Thomas F. Magner. Columbus, Ohio: Slavica Publishers, Inc., 1978.

Rieth, N. *Die geographische Verbreitung des Deutschtums in Rumpf-Ungarn.* Stuttgart: 1927.

Rippley, La Vern J. *The German-Americans.* New York: University Press of America, 1984.

Rohán, A.B. *Prinz Eugen, Ein Donauschwäbische Gedenkschrift.* Wien, 1963.

Rohr, Robert. *Unser Klingendes Erbe.* Passau: Passavia Druckerei GmbH, Verlag Passavia Passau, 1988.

Rohrbacher, Leopold. *Ein Volk - Ausgelöscht: Die Ausrottung des Donauschwabentums in Jugoslawien 1944-48.* Eigenverlag Leopold Rohrbacher, Oberösterreichischer Landesverlag, Betrieb Ried im Innkreis. Herausgegeben vom Forschungsinstitut für Fragen der Heimatlosen im Eigenverlag des Autors. Salzburg, IGN.HARRER. STRASSE #2 , August 1949.

_____. *Die Ausrottung der deutschsprachigen Minoritat in Jugoslawien in den Jahren von 1944 bis 1948.* Eigenverlag Leopold Rohrbacher, Oberösterreichischer Landesverlag, Betrieb Ried im Innkreis. Herausgegeben vom Forschungsinstitut für Fragen der Heimatlosen im Eigenverlag des Autors. Salzburg, IGN. HARRER. STRASSE #2 , August 1949.

Rothenberg, Gunther Erich. *The Austrian Military Border in Croatia, 1522-1747.* Bundesministerium fur Vetriebene, Flüchtlinge und Kreigsgeschädigte, Bonn.

Rothschild, Joseph. *East Central Europe between the Two World Wars.* Seattle: University of Washington Press, 1988.

Royko, Mike. *Boss: Richard J. Daley of Chicago.* New York: E.P. Dutton & Co., Inc., 1971.

Sallet, Richard. Translated by La Vern J. Rippley and Armand Bauer. *Russian-German Settlements in the United States.* Fargo, N.D.: North Dakota Institute for Regional Studies, 1974.

Schapsmeier, Frederick H. and Edward L. Schapsmeier. *Dirksen of Illinois: Senatorial Statesman.* Urbana: University of Illinois Press, 1985.

Schechtman, Joseph B. *Postwar Population Transfers in Europe 1945-1955.* Philadelphia: University of Pennsylvania Press, 1962.

_____. *The Refugee in the World.* Philadelphia: University of Pennsylvania Press.

_____. "The Elimination of German Minorities in Southeastern Europe". Journal of Central European Affairs, July 1946.

Schelbert, Leo. with Hedwig Rappolt. *Alles ist ganz anders hier: Auswandererschicksale in Briefen aus zwei Jahrhunderten.* Freiburg im Breisgau: Walter-Verlag, 1979.

_____. "Vevay, Indiana, and Chabag, Bessarabia: The Making of Two Winegrower Settlements". *Yearbook of German-American Studies*, Vol. 25, (1990), pps. 109-129.

Scherer, Anton. *Die Nicht Sterben Wollten: Donauschwäbischen Literatur von Lenau bis zur Gegenwart.* Donauschwäbisches Bibliographisches Archiv. Prof. Dr. Anton Scherer, A-8044, Graz- Mariatrost, Postfach. 1985.

_____. *Donauschwäbische Bibliographie, 1935-1955, Das Schrifttum über die Donauschwaben in Ungarn, Rumaenian, Jugoslawien und Bulgarian sowie-nach 1945- in Deutschland, Österreich, Frankreich, USA, Canada und Brasilien.* München: Verlag des Südostdeutschen Kulturwerks, 1966.

Schieder, Theodor. "Die Ostvertreibung als wissenschaftliches Problem", *Vierteljahresheft für Zeitgeschichte*, Stuttgart: Deutsche Verlags-Anstalt, 1.Heft, Januar, 1960.

Schumacher, Ludwig. *Die Wirtschaftskraft der Banater Schwaben.* Stuttgart: 1954.

Schunemann, Konrad. *Österreiches Bevolkerungs unter Maria Theresia.* Berlin: Deutsche Rundschau, 1935.

Senz, Josef Volkmar. with Anton Tafferner and Josef Schmidt. *Geschichte der Donauschwaben.* Donauschwäbisches Archiv, Reihe III/ Band 37, München, 1987, Offsetdruckerei E. Beck, Straubing.

_____. with Anton Tafferner and Josef Schmidt. *The Danube-Swabians in the Pannonian Basin, A New German Ethnic Group.* Straubing: Offsetdruckerei E. Beck, 1981.

Seton-Watson, Hugh. *The Sick Heart of Modern Europe: The Problem of the Danubian Lands.* Seattle: University of Washington Press, 1975.

_____. *The East European Revolution.* New York: Frederick A. Praeger Pub., 1951.

_____. *Eastern Europe Between the Wars, 1918-1941.* New York: Harper Torchbooks, Harper & Row, Pub., 1967.

Smith, Glenn II. *Langer of North Dakota: A Study in Isolationism 1940-1959*: New York: Garland Pub., Inc., 1979.

Spira, Thomas. "German-Hungarian Relations and the Swabian Problem, From Károlyi to Goemboes, 1919-1936". *East European Quarterly*, New York: Columbia University Press, 1977.

Springenschmid, Karl. *Our Lost Children: Janissaries?* Translated by John Adam Koehler and Eve Eckert Koehler. Milwaukee: Danube-Swabian Association of the USA, Inc., Schmidt Brothers Printing Co., 1980.

Stanglica, Franz. *Die Auswanderung der Lotharinger in das Banat und die Batschka im 18 Jahrhundert.* Frankfurt a.M.: Elsass-Lothringen Institut, 1934.

Steigerwald, Jacob. *Reflections of the Danube-Swabians in America.* Winona, Minn.: Winona State University Press, 1983.

_____. *Tracing Romania's Heterogeneous German Minority From Its Origins To The Diaspora.* Winona, Minn.: Winona State University Press, 1985.

Straka, Manfred. "Das Südostdeutschtum als Europäisches Aufbauelement". *Eigentumer und Verleger: Österreich Landsmannschaft.* Wein: December,1964.

Swanstrom, Edward E. *Pilgrims of the Night.* New York: Sheed and Ward, 1950.

_____. "The Expellees and Surplus Population". Speech given at the A.A.S. Banquet, Dec.10,1950. American Aid Society Museum, Lake Villa, Illinois.

Sweet, Paul R. "Prince Eugene of Savoy: Two New Biographies". *Journal of Modern History*, June 1966.

Taylor, A.J.P. *The Course of German History.* New York: Capricorn Books, 1962.

Teleki, Paul. *The Evolution of Hungary and its Place in European History.* New York: Macmillan, 1923.

Turcke, K.E. *Das Schulrecht der Deutschen Volksgruppen in Ost und Südost Europa.* Berlin, 1938.

Viorst, Milton. *Hustlers and Heroes: An American Political Panorama.* New York: Simon and Schuster.

von Farkas, Julius. *Die Kultur der Ungarn.* Konstanz: Akademische Verlagsgesellschaft, Athension, 1962.

von Kerney, Franz. *The Danube-Swabian Story: A Century of Achievement and Injustice.* Copyrighted 1988 by Frank Schmidt, 1 Lyme Regis Crescent, Scarborough, Ontario, Canada M1M 1E3.

Walter, Elizabeth B. *Barefoot in the Rubble.* Palatine, Illinois: Pannonia Press, 1997.

Weidlein, Johann. *Ungarns Revisionspolitik und der Untergang des Deutschen Reiches.* Schorndorf: Buchdruckerei Adolf Haushahn.

_____. *Der Prozess gegen Dr. Franz Anton Basch.* Schondorf: 1956.

Wertheimer, Mildred. *The Pan-German League, 1890-1914.* New York: Columbia University, 1924.

Wessely, Kurt. "Die Österreichische Militärgrenze", *Der Gottinger Arbeitskreis, Heft 43*, Kitzingen-Main, Holzner Verlag, 1954.

Willett, Ralph. *The Americanization of Germany.* London: Routledge Pub., 1992.

Wyman, David S. *Paper Walls: America and the Refugee Crisis, 1938-1941.* Amherst: University of Massachusetts Press, 1968.

Ziemer, Gerhard with Hans Wolf. *Wandervögel und Freideutsche Jugend.* Bad Godesberg: Voggenreiter Verlag, 1962.

DOCUMENTS

Das Shicksal der Deutschen in Jugoslawien. Augsburg: Weltbild Verlag GmbH, 1994. ISBN 3-89350-697-7

Documents made public by the Federal Republic of Germany, (*Bundesministerium für Vertriebene, Flüchtlinge und Kreigsgeschädigte*), concerning the fate of Germans in Yugoslavia after the Second World War. 644 pages. In German.

Das Schicksal der Deutschen in Rumanien. Augsburg: Weltbild Verlag GmbH, 1994. ISBN 3-89350-697-7

Documents made public by the Federal Republic of Germany concerning the fate of Germans in Rumania following the Second World War. 419 pages. In German.

Das Schicksal der Deutschen in Ungarn. Augsburg: Weltbild Verlag GmbH, 1994. ISBN 3-89350-697-7

Documents made public by the Federal Republic of Germany relating to the fate of Germans in Hungary following the Second World War. 203 pages. In German.

German Aid Society Records. Department of Special Collections, Library of the University of Illinois at Chicago.
> A collection of documents, newspaper clippings and case files of the German Aid Society of Chicago.

American Aid Society Documents and Photographs.

> A large amount of letters, official forms, assurances, photographs, official minutes of meetings, financial records, corporate charter records, arrival envelopes and other kinds of documents too numerous to list. Presently located at the American Aid Society Museum, Lake Villa, Illinois and soon to be transferred to the Special Collections Department of the Library of the University of Illinois at Chicago.

American Aid Societies *Bulletin.*

> A selection of this self-published periodical, probably incomplete, dating from 1948 until 1950. Presently located in the American Aid Society Records, Danube Swabian Cultural Center, Lake Villa, Illinois. Soon to be housed at the Special Collections Department of the Library of the University of Illinois at Chicago.

U.S. Congress. Senate. *Hearings Before the Subcommittee of the Committee of the Judiciary on S.1794, S.2113, and S.2149, Bills to Amend the Refugee Relief Act of 1953*. 84th Cong., 1st sess., Washington, D.C.: Government Printing Office, 1955.

U.S. Congress. Senate. "Admission of Jews Into Palestine." *Senate Document No.182.* 79th Congress, 2nd Session, 1946. (Report of the Anglo-American Committee of Inquiry.)

U.S. Congress. Senate. "Displaced Persons," *Hearings Before the Subcommittee of the Committee of the Judiciary on Amendments to the Displaced Persons Act*. 81st Congress, Senate, 1st and 2nd Sessions, 1949-1950.

U.S. Congress. Senate. "Displaced Persons in Europe," Report of the Committee on the Judiciary Pursuant to Senate Resolution 137. *Report No. 950*. 80th Congress, 2nd Session, March 2, 1948.

U.S. Congress. Senate. "Report to the Senate Steering Committee on the Possible Admission of Displaced Persons to the United States," (Revercomb Report). Reprinted in 80 C 1, *Congressional Record* 93(2):2507-20, March 25, 1947.

U.S. Congress. House. Report of a Special Subcommittee of the Committee on the Judiciary, *Expellees and Refugees of German Ethnic Origin*. Report No. 1841, 81st Congress, 2nd Session. Washington, D.C.: Government Printing Office, 1950.

U.S. Congress. House. "Proceedings of the National Resettlement Conference for Displaced Persons," *House Document No. 220,* 81st Congress, 1st Session. Washington D.C.: Government Printing Office, 1949.

U.S. Congress. House. "Amending The Displaced Persons Act of 1948." *House Report No. 581.* 81st Congress, 1st Session, 1949.

U.S. Congress. House. "Amending the Displaced Persons Act of 1948." *Hearings Before Subcommittee No.1 of the Committee of the Judiciary on H.R. 1344.* 81st Congress, 1st Session, 1949.

U.S. Congress. House. "Displaced Persons and the International Refugee Organization," *Report of a Special Subcommittee of the Committee on Foreign Affairs.* 80th Congress, 1st Session, 1947.

U.S. Congress. House. "The Displaced Persons Analytical Bibliography," *House Report No. 1687.* Prepared by a special subcommittee of the Judiciary Committee. February 27, 1950.

U.S. Congress. House. *Hearings Before the President's Commission on Immigration and Naturalization.* 82nd Congress, 2nd Session. Committee on the Judiciary, September 30, 1952-October 29, 1952.

U.S. Congress. House. "Permitting Admission of 400,000 Displaced Persons Into the United States," *Hearings Before Subcommittee on Immigration and Naturalization of the Committee of the Judiciary, H.R. 2910.* 80th Congress, 1st Session, June 4-July 18, 1947.

U.S. Displaced Persons Commission. *The Displaced Persons Commission Semiannual Report to the President and the Congress.* February 1, 1949, August 1, 1949, February 1, 1950, August 1, 1950, February 1, 1951, August 1, 1951 Washington, D.C.: Government Printing Office.

Memo to America: The DP Story, The Final Report of the United States Displaced Persons Commission. By John W. Gibson, chairman. Washington, D.C.: Government Printing Office, 1952.

VIDEO TAPES/FILMS

Die Geschicte Der Donauschwaben. Produced and narrated by Adam Albecker, 6 hrs., 1993.
A chronicle of the Donauschwaben in art works of the period and later.

Traudie Müller-Wlossack Interview, (Approx. 38 mins)
An interview with Wlossack featuring documentary footage.

Eve Eckhart Koehler Interview, Produced by Raymond Lohne. (Approx. 3 hrs)
   An interview with Koehler dealing with her life and work.

Survivor's Interviews, Produced by Raymond Lohne. (Approx. 2 hrs.)
   Interviews with Swabian survivors of death-camps in Yugoslavia.

Nick Pesch Films Produced by the American Aid Societies. (Approx. 2 hrs.)
   Various films made by Nick Pesch in Europe in 1949.

American Aid Societies Films, Produced by the American Aid Societies. (approx. 2 hrs.)
   Various films made by the A.A.S. covering special events, festivals and member excursions.

German-Hungarian Old People's Home Film, Produced by the German Hungarian Old People's Home Society. (30 minutes.)
   A film made in 1936 showing the grand opening of the German-Hungarian Old People's Home in Lake Villa.

AUDIO TAPES

Richard Gunther Interview. Produced by Raymond Lohne. (approx. 2 hrs.)
   An audio interview with Richard Gunther on the origins of the A.A.S. and his role in the rescue effort.

Helen Meiszner Interview. Produced by Raymond Lohne. (approx. 1 hr.)
   An audio interview with Helen Meiszner regarding the role of the Meiszner family in the rescue work of the A.A.S.